VICTORIAN DAYS IN ENGLAND

Anna Maria Fay in later life.
Photograph kindly supplied by Fan Hillsmith, a great niece of Anna Maria Fay

Victorian Days in England

**Letters home by an American girl
1851-1852**

by Anna Maria Fay

*with additional material by
Julia Ionides and Peter Howell*

The Dog Rose Press
Ludlow
England
2002

Victorian Days in England
by Anna Maria Fay
A facsimile reprint
First published in 1923
in Cambridge, USA

with additional material
by Julia Ionides and Peter Howell

Copyright © 2002

Peter Howell and Julia Ionides
The Dog Rose Press
26 Bell Lane
Ludlow
Shropshire SY8 1BN

The additional material designed and set in
Optima by the Dog Rose Press.
This font was designed by Herman Zapf

Printed and bound by Biddles Limited, Guildford

Printed and published in the United Kingdom
Date of publication 2002.

ISBN 0-9528367-2-6

PREFACE AND ACKNOWLEDGEMENTS

by Julia Ionides

It was a lucky chance that brought us to Anna Maria Fay. A page of her book was given to us by an architectural historian friend and we liked it so much we decided to look for a copy when we went to America. We stayed in Cambridge, Massachusetts for a week and walked around the area looking at the colleges and buildings. We did not realise, until we went to New York and bought a copy of *Victorian Days in England*, that we had been walking past the house once owned by Judge Samuel Prescott Phillips Fay, Anna Maria's grandfather. We were fortunate to return there two years later and went to Fay Hall, as it is now known, and searched in the library for information about the house and the Fay family.

The 150th anniversary of Anna Maria's visit to England falls this year and the exhibition to celebrate this event, put on by the Richard's Castle Historical Society, proved to be the opportunity we had been waiting for to republish the book of her letters. We also decided to add information about the families and houses that she visited, as well as photographs of the buildings. We are very grateful to all the owners for allowing us to take photographs of their houses which have helped to build up the images of the world Anna Maria describes so well: Viscount Windsor Mr and Mrs Mark Wiggin, Mr Robin Parish, Mrs Lumsden, Dr Martin Speight and Mr and Mrs Acton. Thanks are also due to Mr Tom Wall, Mr Tony Carr of the Shropshire Research and Record

Research and Record Centre, the Richard's Castle Historical Society, Ludlow Museum and to Terry Stone for once more proof reading for us.

Anna Maria brought a lively fresh approach to the rather staid society around Ludlow at that time. All was new to her and she lost no time in recording it. She delighted in the stately dinner parties, observing all the details to relay to her family at home, but she was also just as perceptive when describing the stops on the organ in Ludlow Church. She was present at notable events such as the opening of the railway line from Shrewsbury to Ludlow. She makes an excellent eye witness to the life around Ludlow of 1851-2.

When we first looked at the Fay Family Website we realised what a large and interesting family they are, but without the help of Linda Fay Kaufman and her speedy responses we would have found it hard to negotiate the extensive site and it would all have taken much longer. Thanks to her also for letting us use the biographical research material she has put together and for writing the introduction. We are grateful to Frank and Jervis Janney for sending information and the photograph of the portrait of Clara Fay. The information received from Woods Hole Historical Collection, Massachusetts, The Houghton Library, Harvard, and The Radcliffe Archives, Cambridge, Massachusetts, has helped to bring the Fay family to life for us and we hope that it will for you also.

THE FAY FAMILY IN THE UNITED STATES

By Linda Fay Kaufman

The American Fay family began in 1656 when John Fay, a lad of 8 years arrived in the *Speedwell* from England. It is not known whether he was travelling alone or with an adult; he may have been joining a relative here. There is, as is usual in such things, evidence pointing both ways. The history of the family before John, the origin of the name, the possible connection with Huguenot migrations—all this belongs at the moment to the realm of speculation, propped up though it may be by bits and pieces of evidence. What happened to John Fay once he arrived here is less open to conjecture, in large part because of the work of Fay, Morse, and Spooner, *u.a.*, work which found its proper form in the publication of a book, *John Fay of Marlborough and his Descendants,* in 1898, by Orlin Prentice Fay. Most of the present day knowledge of the family extends Orlin's researches.

Early Fays, establishing themselves firmly on a Massachusetts base, devoted themselves to land and learning, to politics and public service, to manufacturing and, when the times required it, to military service. Many sacrificed their lives for causes they considered to be just. Independence and freedom from outside control in the Revolutionary War, the abolition of slavery and maintenance of the union in the Civil War, the defence of America in the War of 1812; all brought opportunity for such service. The Battle of Bennington, though well known, is not the only battleground which has seen Fays in combat.

In their search for independence and freedom, for opportunity and new fields (literally and figuratively), they travelled further, into the contiguous states of Vermont, New York, New Hampshire and Connecticut, and then west and south. Fays often appear among the first settlers to open up the frontiers: Ohio, Iowa, Wisconsin, Illinois, Michigan, and west to California and Oregon; Fays travelled with their families or alone. Land was bought and passed on within the family; hard work made it productive.

In choosing their wives, Fays seem to have chosen well. The early New England families contributed strong women to the growing Fay family: Brigham, Shattuck, Morse, Hutchinson, Bemis, Child, Spooner; an impressive list even shortened to this extent. Similarly, Fay women married into these same families, bringing the Fay strengths and virtues to them. Orlin Fay's praise of such women concentrates on their devotion to family, their Christian patience and submission, their moral attitude and economy (he was, after all, a man of his times; of one Fay he wrote (p. 147), "best of all, he was a Christian; an avowed, aggressive, consistent Christian."). He is, however, also quick to recognize the intellectual achievements of those who entered the field of education, as did many. The Fay School in Massachusetts is just one early example.

Fay men appear among the graduates of Harvard, Yale, Princeton, Williams, and many other educational institutions. Fays are to be found among the rolls of local officials, frequently extending their influence over a larger area and constituency by election or appointment. One of the characteristics mostly frequently noted by their biographers is integrity, and this quality seems to have colored all of their political service, whether it was on the conservative or more liberal side. Orlin Fay's summary of Francis Ball Fay might be used to illustrate not only Orlin's view of this individual but also many of the qualities so highly prized by Fays in general.

> *He was emphatically a 'self made man,' keen in his judgments, successful in business, respected and honored in the several communities in which he lived, social, genial, intelligent and honest. His early want of opportunity for acquiring knowledge was always regretted and he never ceased to be a student. At fifty years of age he applied himself under private instruction to the study of English and Latin grammar (p. 295).*

The Fay branch into which Anna Maria was born was more prosperous than most. The career of her grandfather, Judge Samuel Prescott Phillips Fay increased the family reputation for honesty, integrity and fidelity, while also increasing his personal worth. The 1850 census lists his occupation as "Judge of Probate" and the value of the real estate he owns as $7,500: a large sum indeed for that day. His seven children added to the prosperity into which they were born. Maintaining their residences in and around Boston, these recognized the value of land and bought and built. It is interesting to note in this respect that Anna Maria reported her occupation for the 1900 census as "capitalist." (In the 1920 census, no occupation is given.) Woods Hole became a favourite area for these Fays, and large houses were built, and land developed. Joseph Story's experiments with replanting forests on sandy soil illustrate the Fay care for property and land. Other members of this group left Massachusetts and headed west, carrying with them the same qualities that had been responsible for their success in Massachusetts.

Anna Maria Fay's strengths in writing and her powers of observation bring to mind other Fays whose writings have come to us; Orlin Fay, of course, but also Peter Fay of Southborough, who in writing of Southborough passed on much valuable information on the Fays; and James M. G. Fay of Vermont, whose Fay Papers, located in Bennington, show wit and knowledge. Unlike them, she seems to have been writing for family rather than a wider circle; but the skill with pen and the devotion to language are qualities she shares with them.

Her place in literature is now as firm as her place in the Fay Family of Massachusetts.

Portrait of Clara Fay by her husband, Frank Hill Smith

VICTORIAN DAYS
IN ENGLAND

LETTERS OF AN AMERICAN GIRL

1851–1852

BY

ANNA MARIA FAY

BOSTON AND NEW YORK

HOUGHTON MIFFLIN COMPANY

The Riverside Press Cambridge

1923

The Riverside Press

CAMBRIDGE · MASSACHUSETTS

PRINTED IN THE U.S.A.

PREFACE

It may be interesting to the reader of these letters, written more than seventy years ago, to know something of the writer, Miss Anna Maria Fay. She was born in Savannah, Georgia, March 12, 1828. Her father was the son of Judge Samuel Prescott Phillips Fay and his wife, Harriet Howard, of Boston. Judge Fay was a native of Concord, but after his marriage his home was in Cambridge, the later years of his life being spent in the house which is now known as Fay House, Radcliffe College. At an early age their eldest son, Samuel Howard, went to Savannah and became prominently identified with the banking and mercantile affairs there. He married Susan Shellman, the daughter of John Shellman and Clarissa Montfort, German and French Huguenots.

Anna Maria's early years were passed in Savannah in happy surroundings. At eleven she was placed in a school at Montpelier, Georgia, under the charge of English teachers, where she remained for five years. The family then came north to live, first in New Haven and later in New York. For a year she was at St. Mary's Hall, Barrington, New

Jersey, then under Bishop Doane's supervision. There her school days ended. Later, however, she had the companionship of a Shakespearean scholar, and with daily access to a good library her education may be said to have been continued.

In 1851, by the invitation of her uncle, Mr. Richard Fay, of Boston, she and her aunt, Maria D. Fay, of Cambridge, spent a year in England at a countryseat in Shropshire leased by Mr. Fay. This estate, known as the Moor Park, was not far from Ludlow Castle, where Milton's "Comus" was performed in 1634. It was in a delightful English countryside near the borderland of Wales, where the English country life could be seen to the best possible advantage. As shown by her letters, their English neighbors received them with marked cordiality and paid them every possible attention.

After her return from England she lived with her family in New York. Here her aunt, Mrs. Henry W. Hills, a woman of remarkable charm and intellect, gathered about her all that was best in the world of literature, music, art, and diplomacy, and at her receptions Miss Fay met many of the most interesting men and women of the day.

In 1880 Miss Fay and her mother moved to Boston. A year later, upon the death of her sister, Mrs. Frank Hill Smith, she assumed the care and direction of her home and children. The last years of her life were passed within the limits of her own home, and in her ninety-fourth year she died. Although in her later years her failing eyesight curtailed her reading, she always retained her interest in the life about her and her sympathies were ever ready for those who sought them.

R. H. S.

E. H. S.

Boston, *March*, 1923

CONTENTS

CONTENTS xi

VICTORIAN DAYS
IN ENGLAND

I

THE WHITE LION INN
SHREWSBURY, *Nov.* 1, 1851
Seven of the clock

MY DEAR H——:

I foresee the astonishment with which you will read this page and the place from which I write. It is hardly greater than that which we feel in being here, yet I do not mean to gratify your curiosity without describing first our disembarkation, our arrival in Liverpool, our adventures there, and then you will appreciate the romance of my writing to you from the White Lion Inn in the old town of Shrewsbury, by whose clock Jack Falstaff "fought the long hour." Train's Agent took off my letter to my mother before I could sign my name (you could not doubt whence it came) or tell her that the same person brought us three letters from Uncle Richard, the first saying that he should leave the Moor Park on the 23rd, the second that he was about to leave, and the third that he had actually been in Liverpool since the 23rd. Of course we were delighted, and waited with great impatience to get aboard the Custom House Barge, which was to take us ashore.

At twelve o'clock finally, after great delay, we got on the funniest, most old-fashioned little steamer, which took sufficiently long to land to give us a view of the wonderful Liverpool docks. Placed ashore, our first aim was the Custom House, whither our baggage followed, we trudging on in front a short distance through wet streets and muddy sidewalks, until we found ourselves within the dreaded abode where a huge sign indicated the office of the "searcher." Maria's baggage and mine were the first to be examined, and I must say that John Bull was most lenient, merely passing in a gentle manner his hands around the sides of the trunks and disturbing nothing. In the meantime Mr. Thayer (Train's Agent) had met us and informed us that Uncle Richard, after waiting five days had gone off, worn out, and left orders for us with Baring Brothers. Now the plot thickens, and now come the adventures!

The Captain proposed to go with us at once to the Barings'. Accordingly, we bade everybody farewell, Colomb and all, and followed the Captain in a cab with our four trunks, two hat-boxes, two carpetbags, stowed inside and out. We went first to Mr. Train's office, where a brisk young man cashed our bill of exchange, then to that of Baring Brothers. Mr. Baring was sent for and came smilingly forward, regretting that he could not induce

Mr. Fay to remain, and to our anxious inquiry
about the directions left for us he replied that he
had none. Imagine our blank astonishment. He
did not even know where Ludlow was, but said he
would be happy to do anything for us that he could.
However, we came to the conclusion that we
could do nothing better than go to the Adelphi,
where Uncle Richard had directed us to meet
him.

Accordingly, the Captain put us into a cab again
and we set off by ourselves for the hotel, not
frightened, but infinitely amused at being in Liverpool in such a predicament. At the hotel we found
letters giving us most minute directions in case we
would not wait until Uncle Richard came for us.
We did not observe that he said we must leave in
the morning, nor did we appreciate how far we had
to go, so we decided to start at three o'clock. In
the meantime we were shown into a parlor, where
we ordered a dinner at two o'clock and having
warmed ourselves at a good coal fire we proceeded
upon our shopping excursion. On leaving the Adelphi, fine streets opened on every side, built up with
handsome substantial brick and stone buildings,
and the streets filled with short fat men in short
coats and short fat women in short petticoats, and
those held up to the knees. We were in such spirits
that all the way down the street we kept saying,
"What a joke, what a joke!"

The sight of the shops had such an effect upon

Maria that I had to drag her along, else she would have bought up all Liverpool. Having made our purchases, the first of which was an umbrella (for it rains every five minutes in this climate) and the Irish bog chain which I send you, I succeeded in getting Maria back to the hotel, where we found in our snug little parlor covers (mark, covers) laid for two. Oh! the delight of the moment when we sat down to our fried sole, served on a plated dish, with everything about the table either of silver or plate. Then, after having dispatched that course with wonderful relish, we had placed before us an English beefsteak delightfully cooked. For dessert damson tarts and two little glasses of jelly finished our dinner, for all of which, when the bill was presented upon a silver tray, we paid seven shillings. Thus occupied, time soon passed, and our four trunks, our two hat-boxes, our two carpetbags being again stowed in and out of the cab, we set out for the ferryboat which was to take us to Birkenhead on the other side of the river.

Such a coil as was there! Two porters were a-cussin' and a-swearing over our baggage, and finally one of them taking it and running with it ever so far down to the boat and then coming back and taking some more and telling us to follow, and getting out of the way before we could find the money to pay the cabman. Then Maria, seizing her hat-box and rushing distractedly after him, leaving me to open the umbrella, to hold on to my bonnet, my veil, my mantilla, my shawl, and reaching the boat at last with the rain pouring down and the sun shining.

Arrived at Birkenhead, we went in file to pass on our baggage, and in sheer despair I handed the man the purse, to his amusement, and asked him to take out what was necessary. At last, seated in a most comfortable car containing four others besides ourselves, we began the journey to Shrewsbury with the anticipation of reaching there by half-past five, where we hoped that an omnibus! would be found to take us twenty-five miles to Overton Gate, thence some conveyance would carry us to the Moor Park! When the impracticability of the plan occurred to us, we calmly decided to pass the night at the White Lion, where Uncle Richard directed us to take the coach, determining, if no coach could be found to take us to-morrow (Sunday), to wait patiently until Monday.

And now our minds being relieved on that point, we set to work to admire everything we saw. It would be impossible for me in this short space to do justice to the wonderful solidity of the railways, the absence of dust, the elegance of the large depots and the prettiness of the small ones, the beauty of the country, the lovely hedges, the picturesque cottages scattered on every side, the air of culture, of content, of prosperity, that met us everywhere — the cultivated hills, the beautiful bridges that span the charming little streams, and the odd English and Welsh names that the men called out at every station. Everywhere was order, no hustling, no noise, but respect and attention from all.

At half-past five we arrived at Shrewsbury with just light enough left to observe that we were being carried by an omnibus through narrow, old-fashioned streets with quaint old houses overhanging us, and finally being landed before a queer antique Inn and being ushered through an intricate hallway till we found ourselves facing our landlady whose portly form obstructed the passage. Preceded by mine hostess, we mounted old oak stairs, turned odd corners, and finally found ourselves in the sweetest little parlor with our bedroom adjoining. Imagine us in a five-cornered room, of which the fireplace occupied one side — the sea-coal fire that burned in the grate, the little mantelpiece adorned with little old-fashioned jars and surmounted by a plain glass; then the bay window, facing the door, with its white linen shades, the tempting couch so neatly covered with chintz, the comfortable armchair by the fireplace, the little old-fashioned sideboard facing the table where I sit, upon which, under a glass case and staring at me with its great round eyes, is a stuffed owl. Beside and around him are placed old English china and glass. On another table stand two plated astral lamps, a silver tray, and some castors. On the walls, covered with quaint paper, and close to the low ceiling are some oil landscapes, two engraved portraits of Doctors and an engraving of Leonardo da Vinci dying in the arms of Francis the First.

If the charm of the scene be not complete, imagine us at tea, Maria seated before the little tray containing a diminutive tea-set with tiny cream pot, filled with the best cream, quaint china cups and saucers and plates, two covered dishes containing hot muffins and cakes, a little glass tub half filled with watercresses upon which is laid the butter; orange marmalade and a loaf of bread, with the water pot hissing on the fire, complete the scene.

The bedroom is equally comfortable and queer, the bed hung with chintz curtains, and the little bureau and etceteras of a bedroom. Oh, that you were here, how much more could I enjoy it! I think of you all in everything I see, in everything I feel or enjoy.

Fortunately, the mail coach goes to-morrow morning, at four o'clock, to Ludlow, and Boots is to call us. We shall arrive at Ludlow in time for breakfast. Only think of it! After all, it was much better that we should come on here. I am sure you will agree with me in thinking that everything has been done for us that could have been done.

Good-bye, until we get to the Moor Park. If you all were only going to be there!

MOOR PARK, *November 3rd*

WHERE am I to begin! I left off writing, tired and ready to go to bed, and after a sleepless night got up in time to be ready for the coach at half-past four, and more than an hour before "The uprisen sun peered forth the golden window of the East." Notwithstanding the rain and the darkness, we discerned that our coachman was the personification of Mr. Weller — great red cheeks and a bottle nose.

We passed through the ancient and picturesque town of Shrewsbury without being able to see a thing, and it was some time before there was light enough to see anything but the hedges by the side of the road. Finally, however, the light came and with it such scenes! Every cottage a picture, every landscape a poem! For twenty miles we drove through what appeared to us Paradise. Parks on all sides with sheep and cattle grazing under magnificent oaks, mountains in the distance tinted under a glorious rising sun with shades of purple, cottages sometimes in the foreground, sometimes on hillsides, in valleys, built of stone with pointed thatched roofs and the fronts and sides covered with ivy or flowering vines — such was the country through which we approached the Moor Park: sometimes passing through antique little villages whose narrow streets and projecting and ornamented house fronts reminded us of stage scenes, sometimes catching a glimpse of the Gothic tower covered with ivy of the parish church, while now and then the still Sunday morning air would bear to us some distant chime.

If I were to attempt to tell you all I saw and all I enjoyed, in landscapes, in wonderful atmospheric effects, and to describe all the lovely lodges and cottages we passed, I should never have done. Suffice it to say that at last we reached Ludlow, yet more antique if possible than anything we have seen, and the coach put us down before the Angel Inn. Here a fly or cab was soon got ready to take us over to the Moor. It was now half-past eight o'clock, and the villagers began to make their appearance, the men in clean white smock frocks which have excited our admiration, but which I must not stop to describe.

A drive of two miles and a half, through the same lovely scenes brought us to the Lodge gates, and now imagine the excitement with which we drove through the avenue shaded by lofty oaks, with sometimes a lovely lawn on one side and a dell on the other, and glimpses of landscape breaking through the groups of trees. At last the house came in sight, built of brick, covered here and there with ivy and other vines. The front door at last reached, eager faces were looking out, and in another moment the carriage door and the hall door being simultaneously opened, we were received with the most affectionate and hearty welcome from Uncle Richard and Aunt Catherine, and by the children with an ardor and enthusiasm not to be equalled.

We were not long in getting into the hall, and

thence through the library into the breakfast room, where breakfast was just ready. We were overwhelmed with affectionate inquiries and anxieties about our voyage and health. Aunt Catherine is the picture of health — she has grown just stout enough — while Uncle Richard seems very well and happy. Kitty and Lily are the fairest creatures I ever saw, and the pictures of health, and lovely, not only in person, but charming in manner and perfect in dispositions. Willie is the counterpart of Richard in manner and appearance. He claimed me at once for Bobby and himself. You cannot imagine anything more delightful than to be received as we were. A note of welcome from Richard, as you would imagine he would write, was there instead of himself, and your letter gave me unspeakable pleasure and only made me wish the more that you were here.

And now I must begin to describe the house. The Moor belongs to a family named Salway, and I must quote what Burke says of them: "The Sewyin, or Salways, are of Saxon origin and were settled at Cannoc (the present Kanke) in the County of Stafford, at a period antecedent to the Conquest. Thence they spread into Worcestershire, Salop, and other shires, and have been resident at Richard's castle, Shropshire, for several generations. The first of the family, Jeoffrey de Salway, held lands in Norton-under-Cannoc, in the County of Stafford, under Henry III, 1216. They have always held honorable positions in their day. The present proprietor is John Salway, who, from extravagance, finds it necessary to economize."

Now, to describe the house. You enter a very large square hall, panelled with oak to the ceiling, and the floor is of marble. In the centre stands a billiard table; opposite the front door and at the end of the hall near the broad open staircase is a great screen, so quaint that I shall copy it some day. Around the walls hang the ancestors, prim gentlemen in wigs and stiff ladies in brocades. A fireplace is at one side where these ancient ladies and gentlemen sat in front of blazing logs, but for which their posterity have substituted a black stove. From the hall on one side you enter the library, in which, as Uncle Richard says, Addison is a modern writer. However, it is filled with rare editions of old authors. Adjoining the library is the dining-room — a large room, once a servants' hall, but in modern times lined with oak and converted to its present purpose. On the walls hang some fine portraits; the room otherwise is perfectly simple, containing merely the accessories of the dinner table—an oaken board at the end of the room instead of a buffet, etc. This completes the rooms on one side of the hall.

On the other are the drawing-rooms, quite modern in furniture. The front room is not used in winter probably; the back room, into which it enters by folding doors, is our sitting-room, the windows of which command a lovely view of which, when I have time, I will send sketches. The two windows of the room are hung with red curtains with white undercurtains. The walls are papered with red and yellow paper, the furniture is covered with red. In front of the table where I sit is a case reaching to the ceiling in which are placed some curious stuffed birds and a wild-cat (killed on the estate), in glass boxes. From this room you enter a little boudoir; thence a glass door opens into a conservatory which also connects with a little boudoir entering into the front parlor. Ascending by a fine broad staircase, you reach the bedchambers on each side of a long corridor. Uncle Richard's dressing-room is hung with tapestry, and adjoining is a sort of closet, where he says he keeps the pictures of his favorite ancestors. Aunt Catherine's room is handsome, but I do not remember any particulars about it. Our room is entirely Chinese. The walls, the furniture, the china on the washstand, the curtains of the bed and windows are covered with the persons and residences of the inhabitants of the Celestial Empire. Indeed, there is no situation too humble for these exalted personages to occupy.

November 5th

WE have been here quite long enough to feel, as it were, to the Manor born. I walk through the hall and look up at the respectable ladies and gentlemen hanging on the wall as if I could ascribe the twist in my hair to the prim madam in white satin, or the

thinness of my face to the grim gentleman in black.
Farther than this, I should not care to resemble the
defunct ancestors of the Salways, for they are at
best a pug-nosed set. The garden is one of the
loveliest features of the Moor — hothouses filled
with grapes; walls upon which are trained pears,
apricots, figs, peaches, and other fruits; quantities
of flowers are yet in bloom; and game is plenty.
Day before yesterday, Uncle Richard brought home
nine brace of partridges and a hare; yesterday a
pheasant and the first woodcock of the season. He
has besides two miles of fish preserves.   Rooks
and rabbits abound. I have tasted the famous hare
soup, but I think it requires that one should become accustomed to the high game flavor to like it
very much. I drink every day at lunch a glass of
port, and at dinner a large goblet of ale, and I feel
it no more than water. I am sure that every day
I shall grow stout. The household consists of Miss
Dodd, the governess; Fischer — Aunt Catherine's
German maid — the most invaluable person and
the best creature in the world; the butler and a boy
under him; the coachman whose livery is green
coat with gilt buttons, buff breeches, and top boots;
the gardener, the keeper, and the porter, the cham-
bermaid, the laundry-maid, the cook, and the scul-
lion. Uncle Richard does not keep a stud of horses;
only two carriage horses, one of which is a hunter,
and two ponies, one of which I am to ride. In the
kennel are six dogs that I have not yet seen. Uncle

Richard does not pretend to live in much style —
he accepts no invitations to dinner, for he has come
here to be quiet and to get well.

I took cold just before I left the ship and have
had for a day what seems to be an epidemic here —
a face-ache. However, Fischer's excellent care is
rapidly relieving me, and I feel almost well. It takes
one a little time to become accustomed to the cold
halls which it is impossible to warm. I have got for
myself some black silk at Ludlow to make a little
sack to slip on to run through the halls, to be lined
with tweed. My cold has prevented my going to
Mrs. Betton's on Monday night to tea. Mrs. Betton is a sister of Mrs. Salway, and occupies the
adjoining property. She is a very pleasant person.
Maria has gone to-day with Aunt Catherine to pay
a visit to Lady Cuyler, the wife of Sir Charles
Cuyler. I shall have plenty of opportunities.

The great people of the neighborhood are the
Hon. Mr. and Lady Harriet Clive.[1] The latter is
the sister of the late Earl of Plymouth and brought

[1] Lady Harriet Clive was co-heiress with her sister,
the Marchioness of Devonshire, of her brother the Earl of
Plymouth. After the death of Mr. Clive, the Queen in
1855 created Lady Harriet Baroness Windsor (a title
belonging to the Earldom of Plymouth fallen in abey-
ance), the title to descend. Her son, Mr. Robert Clive,
died before his mother and left a posthumous son, the
present Lord Windsor, who has rebuilt Hewell Grange,
the inheritance from his grandmother, and made it a
magnificent residence. (See *Country Life*, August 15, 1903.)

her husband a great fortune. They live at Oakly Park. They are absent at present and have not called, but Lady Harriet wrote Aunt Catherine a very kind note, 'pleading her immediate departure as an excuse for not calling, and assuring her that she would do so when she returns. Aunt Catherine knows almost every one in the neighborhood, and in course of time I shall tell you of them. I have been out driving every day.

Monday we went to Ludlow, it being a Fair-day. You cannot imagine anything so funny. Crowds of quaint-looking people were collected around the market-house to witness the dancing of some young street dancers — two young girls dressed in short dresses and red bodices and two little boys in fantastic costumes. They danced for the amusement of the crowd in the muddy streets, and when they got through went round for the ha'pennies. To this succeeded ballad-singing on the part of a man and a woman — the former in a tolerably good but nasal tone, while the latter indulged her audience in strains not to be envied by the nightingale. They sang quaint old ballads, such as you would find in Percy's "Reliques," and altogether it was almost impossible to believe that we were not looking upon a stage scene.

Ludlow is full of exquisite houses and is quite a large town. Mr. Charlton's residence I will describe in my next, as we are going to see it. The parish church is so old that they do not know the date, and is in the best style of Early English. It is very large. Maria went to church on Sunday, but I did not, so I must leave that for my next. The church in the gift of the Salways is at Richard's castle, and the rector, Mr. Landon, lives only a little way from here. The whole family called upon us yesterday. We have already seen many of them several times, for there are nine children.

November 6th

TIME passes here so quickly and the days are so short that I am surprised that the day for the steamer letters has already arrived. We rise early at half-past seven, have prayers at half-past eight, and breakfast a quarter of an hour later. After breakfast the children go to their schoolroom and Maria gives Kitty a music lesson. Aunt Catherine and I write or sew until eleven or twelve, when we go out driving. Uncle Richard either goes shooting by himself or with Mr. Betton, and sometimes with Sir Charles Cuyler. We lunch when we return, and at six we dine. In the evening we form a very cheerful party by the drawing-room fire, reading, or sewing, or playing games with the children. I am having a bearskin jacket made for my riding-habit — there is no need for a better habit, I assure you.

I have been thinking of taking lessons in water-colors, but I fear it is almost too much — two guineas a term. The price may be only three guineas for the two — in that case I shall not hesitate. We are to know to-day. It is a good style and an excellent master, and he teaches us to paint from nature entirely.

My face-ache is relieved and my cold is much better. Maria is taking her turn with a cold. It is necessary to become acclimated. Uncle Richard and Aunt Catherine have been kindness itself in having everything done to cure my cold as quickly as possible. The next time I write, two weeks hence, I shall be able to describe aristocratic houses, as we are going everywhere to see everything. Tell John I wish he could see the Parish Church at Ludlow. Maria says the singing is good and the organ excellent. There are such lovely little churches around here.

Love to every one.

II

MY DEAR MOTHER:

I should write with renewed pleasure if I knew that you were not anxiously wondering whether I had arrived and whether that arrival had conduced as much to my health and happiness as you hoped. My last letter will have told you of my taking cold, and I fear will have made you anxious unnecessarily, for I have found myself relieved in a wonderfully short time and in a fair way of gaining that twenty pounds after which I have sighed so much. My appetite is unsatiable, and I am mortified to say that I eat until I am ashamed of myself, yet I am still ready to cry — like the leech's daughters — "More, more." I resort to the ignoble excuse, "Aunt Catherine's dinners are so tempting," to cover any unusual consumption of which I may be guilty. However, if it be the means of making me stout and healthy, and restoring me to you looking like an English girl, I think I can bear the mortification.

I do not think that anything has occurred since I last wrote to interest you particularly. Aunt Catherine delayed lionizing until I should get over my cold, and no sooner was I well than Maria and herself were taken. We had on Thursday a charming drive to the Haye Park — a portion of this property and the first residence of the Salways. It is situated at the top of a well-wooded hill and commands a view than which nothing more lovely can be conceived. The hill and woods where the sister was lost and where the whole scene of the play of "Comus" was laid is pointed out to us, for Ludlow is not without its poetic renown. Milton wrote "Comus" here, and it was first enacted at Ludlow Castle, now a picturesque ruin.

The next day we walked to Mary Knoll, two miles and a half from here, and heard that very echo upon which the lady called in vain. Yesterday I took a ride and found the pony all I could desire. This morning Kitty and I, being the only ones well enough, rode into Ludlow to church. As I told you before, in H——'s letter, the church is very old, but of the purest Early English. Unfortunately, the houses are built so closely around it that you can see nothing but the tower until you pass through a narrow alley. Having, however, penetrated by a miserable sidewalk this uninviting entrance, you are amply repaid by the lovely scene before you. The church is built in the form of a cross, the tower being in the centre. The piercings in the windows are in exquisite style, and in the rich but dilapidated tower birds make their nests. The service had already begun when we arrived, so, instead of entering by the main entrance, we went around through a chapel.

The service was very grand and solemn, even more so than our own, the congregation so devout and the responses so full. The pulpit with the reading-desk is nearly in the centre of the nave. The congregation are seated all around the desk, for you see nothing of the chancel — that being divided off from the body of the church by an oaken screen under the organ, in which a door admits you to the choir in the ancient cathedral style. The organ is over against the pulpit at the end of the church. It was presented in the last century by the Earl of Powis, since when additions have been made. It is large and really fine; not over-powerful, but the tones round and full. Tell John I observe that the sesquialtera was particularly good, and that the organ appeared to have quite a variety of stops — that the bass, though not very powerful was good. The organist did not do it justice. The Venite was read, but the Te Deum was chanted to a rather ordinary double chant; the Jubilate and Gloria after each psalm in the Psalter was sung to one of our most familiar chants, but the words were miserably divided, some gabbled over and others drawled out. The chanting is much slower than ours, and the service is read even more slowly than Mr. Littlejohn does. The curate, Mr. Merrick, reads, and Mr. Phillips preaches in a voice exactly like that of Dr. Taylor's.

I am sorry that our Mother Church here is in a deplorable state. Mr. Phillips, the rector, is a miserably low churchman — indeed, they say he is a very bad man, and his face justifies the report. He is so unpopular that the Dissenting chapels and the alehouses are filled on Sundays. In our parish Mr. Landon, the rector at Richard's castle, is even more unpopular than Mr. Phillips. He gives himself up to hunting, shooting, and fishing, and his kitchen, and it is almost impossible to get him to visit a parishioner even *in extremis*. Though his income is eleven hundred pounds a year, at least, he is very much in debt. At Silvington, another parish in the neighborhood, the rector not only drinks to excess, but is otherwise of the most dissolute habits. The bishop can suspend him, but then the application is attended with great expense and trouble. The parish schools are everywhere neglected — no wonder, then, that the rich go to Rome and the poor to Dissent. On Saturday Uncle Richard went over to Sir Charles Cuyler's to shoot, and the party was composed of Sir Charles, Uncle Richard, the Reverend Mr. Landon of our parish, and the rector from another neighboring parish. They got home about eight o'clock, after which, of course, these fox-hunting priests had to dine and prepare for Sunday.

I could not help thinking this morning, as I looked around upon the congregation, how much purer our own church was. Nothing could exceed the solemnity of the scene, the antique roof, the vaulted arches above us, the stained-glass window of some

chapel behind the organ, the noble organ, the rich
screens dividing this portion of the church from
the choir and chapels, the devout poor seated on the
benches in the middle aisle — old men and decrepit
old women leaning on their sticks and looking up so
reverently to the clergyman and helping to follow the clerk with their quavering voices in the
full responses which seemed to roll through the
church. Around the gallery are blackboards
framed in gilt, upon which are painted in yellow
letters bequests from various individuals; among
them, that twelve of the poorest of the parish are
to receive on every Sunday a loaf of bread, and
outside the door in the vestibule are the loaves
ranged along, while the beadle waits to distribute
them.

The beadle is the personification of Mr. Bumble.
He wears a blue coat with a small cape, of which
the collar is red. The coat is trimmed all around
with one row of gold braid. In addition, he wears a
yellow cravat, and this sets off a visage whose ruddy
plump cheeks and still redder pug nose would do
credit to Mr. Bumble himself. He walks around
the church and keeps all bad children in order.
Immediately under the pulpit are four pews lined
with red, in which sit the Mayor and Corporation
in blue silk gowns trimmed with fur, to which the
former adds a red collar. They read the service out
of great red books about eighteen inches long, and
as they marched out of the church in procession

two officials preceded them carrying silver maces. As I looked down into one of these pews, I saw a person sitting there in citizen's dress whose head resembled exactly Colonel Cutler's. I suppose he was a warden.

I cannot sufficiently admire the beauty of the church edifices, the devoutness of the congregation, and the grandeur of the services, so much heightened by the one and the other. You will bemoan with me the miserable state to which her priests are bringing this noble church. No wonder that Rome makes converts and that the ministers of the Pope have assailed a church thus carelessly guarded.

We are destined to know Mr. Landon's family very well, seeing some of them every day. He has nine children, of whom the eldest is a son at Oxford — Henry about twenty-one, Edward sixteen, and a nephew named Charles are at home studying under a tutor, Mr. Ogle, also a young man. So we shall not be without beaux — they are here every day and walk out with us, and make themselves useful in every way they can. Their sister Janet is neither pretty nor interesting, but both good and amiable. They live at Batchcott, about a quarter of a mile from the Moor, and are our nearest neighbors.

The Bridges live at a place called the Lodge. There are three young ladies in the family, but they are dreadfully stiff, live, eat and drink by rule, and are not at all interesting, they say. They have just lost a relative, so I have not seen them. Mrs.

Betton we see very often, and she is very pleasant, but she has no children. Mr. Betton is very accomplished and very agreeable. Sir Charles Cuyler lives eleven or twelve miles off. He has eleven or twelve children, of whom several are young ladies. They have not yet called upon us.

Wednesday, November 12th

YESTERDAY we went to the Haye Park to see the meet, which we lost by being too late, so for some time we raced about hearing the hounds in full bay and catching a glimpse of a horseman in a red coat, often excited by the cry of "Tally-ho," believing that the fox was coming towards us, and as often disappointed. At last the unhappy fox was caught in the Comus wood without our seeing the sport. Soon, however, the sportsmen began to appear, and they informed us that they were going to draw the covers at the Haye Park. So we followed and had a capital view of them, men, horses, and dogs on the lawn. There were about thirty persons in the field, but no more than five or six gentlemen — the rest were farmers. Among these only two or three were well mounted: Mr. Keville-Davis, of Croft Castle, in red coat, white breeches, and top boots, on a very fine black hunter; Mr. Stubbs on another capital horse. Out of the thirty, not more than six were in red coats. There were seventeen couples of beautiful hounds.

It seemed to me that the sport was very tame,

for the covers and woods were so thick and the country so hilly that the sportsmen were constantly losing the hounds, and the hounds the fox. All they did was to call for the hounds, and to scream "Tally-ho" on the tops of the hills, then perhaps the faint echo of the horn and the bay of the hounds would set them scampering about in all directions, trying in vain to find the hounds. We were at last tired out with dodging about, so we came home, and thus lost a very respectable run.

We spent the evening at Mrs. Betton's, to meet Miss Beale, who is niece to Mrs. Betton, and is there on her way to the ball at Shrewsbury. They say she is five feet eleven tall. At any rate, she looks taller than Uncle Richard, has very light hair, white eyebrows and eyelashes, high cheekbones and a large mouth, and altogether has the air of a person who thinks herself handsome. She is not without style, and sings and plays quite well, but she is so fatiguingly gay that you soon grow tired of her.

November 14th

I HAVE counted the days since you shall have heard from me, and I am sure you must already have received my letter. I was rather disappointed yesterday at not hearing from any of you, although I suppose I ought not to have expected it. I have concluded to take painting lessons. For one lesson a week for both of us, Mr. Gill charges two pounds and three shillings the term. I like his style exceedingly. He came yesterday for the first time. His object is to teach us to sketch from nature in water-colors. He uses moist colors altogether, which only require nine cakes. You cannot imagine anything prettier than the effect he produces by putting colors on tinted paper with a little shading in pencil. I shall take the greatest pleasure in bringing my portfolio well filled with lovely views about Ludlow, for although we shall not be able to take many sketches from nature ourselves, Mr. Gill has himself a great many. I began yesterday upon a view of Ludlow Castle. The three Landons spent the evening here yesterday and we danced at a great rate. I find that they dance the polka, schottische, and Deux Temps very well, indeed.

Sunday, November 16*th*

WE have just returned from church at Ludlow where Aunt Catherine has to perform quite an important office. It is customary that, when a new mayor is elected, on the first Sunday after the election the Archdeacon of Salop preaches a sermon in aid of the Charity Schools, and the collection is taken up at the door, on which occasion it is the etiquette to ask two ladies to hold the plates, or rather the one stands by the Mayor who holds the plate for her, and the other by the ex-Mayor who performs the same office for the other. Aunt Catherine, as a distinguished stranger, was handed

out from the pew just before the Benediction, and
took her position before the door and bowed and
smiled to each one as he or she put money into the
silver plate held by the Mayor. On the other side
of the door was Miss Roche, of Clungunford Hall,
attended, of course, by the ex-Mayor. Aunt Catherine was magnificently dressed in a black velvet
dress and black velvet mantle trimmed with sable.
A bonnet of blue velvet and black lace completed
her very elegant toilette. The Mayor was in his
official dress, which I have previously described.
After the money was counted in the vestry-room —
which amounted to thirty-three pounds and thirteen shillings — which we witnessed, we went to
Mr. Myrick's, the curate and reader, to a very
elegant lunch, where we met a Marquise de Clomat,
the daughter of a Lady Sayre, of Stonehouse; a
Mr. Clarke, a bachelor lawyer of Ludlow; Mr.
Betton, and Mr. Oldham.

While they were counting the money, we had an
opportunity of examining the glorious choir and
chancel, which unfortunately the organ not only
injures but separates from the main body of the
church. Mr. Myrick is going to take us all over the
church sometime. Until then I shall not describe
the choir. Tell John they chanted a Te Deum
which would have been fine if they had not sung so
slowly. I was very much surprised to hear them
sing, to the psalm "Jehovah Reigns," that arrangement from the "Creation" which John uses;

instead of the hymn after the Nicene Creed which comes after the Gospel, they sang what they called an Anthem to the words of the Collect for the seventh Sunday after Trinity. For the Voluntary we had the "Hallelujah Chorus," which the organist played very well — very well, indeed, if I were not accustomed to hear John. The sesquialtera came out with excellent effect, but I must say there is nothing like our trumpet bass. I think I must write to John after I go over the church with Mr. Myrick, for I shall try and get a peep into the organ.

We had a conversation with the beadle, the personification of Mr. Bumble, who, I am happy to say, is more fortunate in his domestic relations than that unfortunate person, having buried his wife. He evidently opposes the papal aggression, for he looked very fierce when he pointed out to us within the chancel rails the place he said where the Roman priest used to stand. Mr. Bumble is a person of limited information, for having acquired a few facts he repeats them by rote, but the moment we questioned him he stood aghast. The Archdeacon preached an excellent sermon, and looked very much like Mr. Charles King.

I have been feeling very anxious for some days for a letter. If I allowed myself to think much about it, I should have been quite homesick and unhappy, but I am surrounded by so much to amuse and interest me that I can always find some-

thing to divert me. I beg that you will make H——
write to me minutely, not in her usual general style,
although I must do her the credit to say that her
first and only letter thus far has been all that I
could desire. I fear you will have cause to complain
of my writing too much. Please give me a hint if
you think so. I must say, however, that my greatest pleasure is to tell you of all that I see and admire.

November 17th, Monday

I HAVE been giving my cheeks a close examination
this morning, and I think I can say confidently
that they are decidedly fuller than when I left
home. Aunt Catherine thinks I have improved
very much since I have been here. My dresses are
getting very tight. I can hardly breathe in my
pink silk. Aunt Catherine has been so unwell with
her cold that we have not been out sight-seeing.
Last evening Mr. Clarke dined here and proposed
to accompany us to an inspection of the castle next
week and to give us a lunch. In my next letter I
propose to send you a history of the castle and
church, which are full of interest. Mr. Myrick is to
take us to see, besides, some curious houses, the
most singular of which is the "Feathers Inn,"
which is renowned for its antique front and beautiful carvings.

The weather has been very cold, indeed. We
found when we arrived snow on the Clee Hills. We

have, however, a most unusual November, fine, clear weather. The sun rises in a cloudless sky, and we gain such confidence in the constancy of fair weather that we no longer take out an umbrella when the sun shines. I think we feel the cold more than we do in America, for it is more penetrating, and though with us the thermometer may be many degrees lower it is more exhilarating. Besides, the houses here are so imperfectly warmed. Aunt Catherine seems to feel the cold terribly, but I think it agrees with me and I do not suffer at all. I have made myself a basquine, and find it very comfortable. Fischer is astonished at my powers, and says — "C'est un amour," so I shall not be "starved with cold," as they say here.

November 18*th*

MARIA and myself, accompanied by Edward and Charles Landon, took a walk of over five miles last evening, and on our return we stopped at a mill to be weighed, and with what pleasure do I tell you that the jolly farmer said I weighed "'at stone," or eight stones. When I asked him how many pounds that was, he said, "A hundred and twelve" — 112. Allowing two pounds for my clogs and extra clothing, it makes five pounds more than I have weighed in a year, and at least seven or eight more than I weighed when I left home. Is not that delightful? "'At stone" is no contemptible weight. Imagine my getting into old-fashioned stilliards and being weighed by the stone! It's the funniest thing in the world to hear the people talk about here. The "h" is left off and put on in the most extraordinary manner. Even an artist like Mr. Gill said to Maria, "I h'advise you to h'invent h'an h'American h'elm." Of course ladies and gentlemen do not talk so, but with the common classes it is carried to such an extent that it is almost impossible sometimes to understand them.

The postbag has just come, and brought me a letter by the American steamer from Ellen, so I am not to hear from you for at least a week to come.

THE CHURCH, TAKEN FROM MR. WRIGHT'S BOOKS

The church at Ludlow is undoubtedly the finest ecclesiastical building in the County of Salop and perhaps the most stately parochial edifice in England, the architecture being in the style of the latter part of the fifteenth century, though it is less florid than is usual in buildings of that period. It is unusually capacious for a parish church, is cruciform in plan, and consists of a nave, choir, chancel, transepts, side aisles, and two large chantry chapels with a finely proportioned and lofty tower in the centre, having at each angle an octagonal turret, surmounted by a pinnacle. In the tower is a melodious peal of eight bells.

The principal entrance from the town is by a large hexagonal porch. The nave is divided from the aisles by six lofty pointed arches on each side, springing from light clustered pillars, each consisting of four taper shafts with intermediate spaces hollowed. Above them is a clerestory with a range of heavy windows devoid of tracery. The great western window is entirely modernized and it is richly ornamented with mullions. The four great arches under the tower are remarkably bold. Beneath the eastern arch is the choral rood loft, the lower part of which is embellished with open carved work, but upon it is erected a modern gallery, above which stands a very fine-toned organ given by Henry Arthur, Earl of Powis, in 1764, and costing one thousand pounds, and has been subsequently enlarged by important additions.

This church having been formerly collegiate was most elegantly fitted up as in cathedrals and has stalls on each side of the choir. These stalls are of excellent workmanship, having been originally intended for the use of ten priests of the rich chantry in the adjoining chapel of St. John of Jerusalem, the Miserere or shelving seats of which exhibit fanciful and grotesque carvings under them. It is not known when the ten priests ceased to officiate in the choral service, though in the register mention is made of the Master of the Choristers (Precentor), a considerable time after the Reformation.

The choir is spacious and lighted by five lofty pointed windows on each side, and one of much larger dimensions at the east end which occupies the whole breadth and nearly the whole height of this part of the building. This great window is entirely filled with stained glass of rich coloring, representing chiefly the legend of St. Lawrence, the patron saint of the church. The whole of the windows in this interesting building bear evidence of having been once enriched with a profusion of stained glass, the splendor of which, judging from what remains, must have been inferior to none in point of coloring, since it appears to have been executed by perfect masters of the art, at a time, too, when glass staining was at its highest perfection, and notwithstanding the defiling hand of time, or more probably the ill-guided zeal of the Puritans, has despoiled the nave of that majestic solemnity and religious awe emanating from the mellowing tints of "storied windows, richly dight."

The choir chancel and chantry chapels, however, retain specimens of no ordinary beauty, where face and figures of no common interest are depicted, though these in places have been so barbarously mutilated by modern repairs as to present a strange mixture of patchwork. (Here I drop Mr. Wright and shall make extracts now and then.)

The great eastern window was so much defaced that it became necessary to restore it. In 1828 the corporation of Ludlow directed Mr. David Evans to restore it according to the original design, and in 1832 it was completed in a manner to excite the admiration of every one at the elaborate skill displayed in restoring and replacing, so that it is impossible to distinguish the old from the new. The window is considered one of the most magnificent specimens of art, and for general effect surpasses anything in the kingdom. It is eighteen feet wide and thirty feet in height and contains five hundred and forty feet of glass in sixty-five compartments.

The subject displayed is the history of St. Lawrence with his miracles and his martyrdom. The whole of the subjects in this window are under elegant canopies of delicate tabernacle work, differing in design, and the costumes of the figures throughout the various scenes are particularly curious. This window is supposed to have been put up in the time of Thomas Spofford, Bishop of Hereford.

The three large windows on each side of the chancel still contain fine specimens of stained glass, and, though the work of the Puritans is very evident, they have left the figures of several bishops and Romish saints. Underneath the eastern window is a modern altar screen in Grecian style and altogether incongruous. The prominent parts are richly gilded, and this, at present, conceals the original one elaborately carved in stone. On the south side of the altar is the piscina and canopied sedilia for the use of priests, deacons, and subdeacons.

The ceiling of this portion of the edifice is of oak, resting on corbels which spring from highly decorated figures of angels bearing shields. The chapels north and south of the choir correspond in size, and are approached from the transept, by remarkably handsome carved screens. The chapel of St. John is north of the choir. In the eastern window are some remnants of stained glass portraying the story of the ring presented by some pilgrims to Edward the Confessor. On the north side is an altar tomb on which rests the finely sculptured figures of Sir John Bridgeman and his wife. Of the south transept and chapel all that is known is that the cordwainers and other companies have from a remote period to the present time continued to meet in them. In this transept is a curious abbreviation of the Decalogue, painted on a large panel, the old text of which has been recently restored. A portion of the stained glass still remains in the eastern window of the south chapel. The chantries were originally endowed with lands for the support of a priest to offer up prayers for the souls of the departed. This use of them was prohibited by Edward the Sixth.

The whole of this noble parish church is ceiled with fine oak and embellished with carvings. The extreme length from east to west is two hundred and three feet, the tower thirty, the choir eighty; the breadth of the aisles and nave is eighty-two feet, length of the transept north and south one hundred and thirty feet, and breadth of the choir twenty-two feet. The tower rises one hundred and thirty

feet, is quadrangular and was originally ornamented with highly finished statues of saints, but
Oliver Cromwell's officers were irreligious and
wicked, and accordingly they either mutilated
them or destroyed them altogether.

There is every reason to suppose that this church
was gradually brought to perfection by a fraternity
of Palmers who have been found attached to it as
far as the history of it can be distinctly traced.
There are quite a number of curious sculptured
tombs and ornamented tombs with highly colored
armorial bearings. The churchyard is full of quaint
tombstones and the readery, or house of the reader
of the service, is almost as curious as the church
itself.

III

MY DEAR H——:

A great weight was lifted from my mind yesterday by the receipt of your letter. I had begun to imagine all sorts of things, notwithstanding Maria's comforting assurance that bad news flies quickly. Your letter was begun, you will find out, the very day we landed at Liverpool. That date is almost the only thing we remember connected with the voyage so completely have more recent pleasures effaced alike its enjoyments and discomforts, except, indeed, that now and then Maria and I hum with a tender melancholy some favorite song of the troubadour's. I am not at all surprised that there is not much incident in N. H. At any rate, whatever there may be you can appropriate entirely to yourself. Fancy having to divide up an incident as the five Miss Cuylers must have to do. To a resident here, Ludlow and its neighboring parks and lodges in which there are always two or three expectant young ladies, must be dull. To me, however, to whom everything is novel, the life is enchanting. The very fact of living where the picturesque forms so completely a part of real life would be happiness enough. Besides, Batchcott

furnishes two willing administrants to my pleasures in Charles and Ned Landon.

Fancy on what easy footing we are that Ned
sent Charles over after luncheon yesterday to say
that he was going to ride to Hanbury for some oats
and that if I would like to go I must be at Batchcott at four o'clock, for he could not come for me,
as he had an engagement from two till four and
daylight was precious. I did not hesitate to accept.
I wonder what my mother would say if she had
known where I was, for, having reached Hanbury
up steep paths, through brush and through briar,
Ned proposed that instead of coming back the
same way we should come back by the Vignyles,
the highest point about here. Lowering clouds
hung over the Clee Hills; the wind whistled as if
to warn us back; darkness was creeping on apace,
and a fine mist moistened my face. But still on we
went through the prickly gorse and over the soft
and slippery turf until, after many hairbreadth
"scapes" from Juliet's stumbling, we reached the
top of the Vignyles with just daylight enough re-
maining to have the most magnificent view of the
vast domains of Downton Castle and the surround-
ing country, while toward the Moor a dense mist
concealed everything from our view. You will be
surprised that I reached home in safety after the
dressing-bell had rung, and in spite of the darkness,
my blindness, and Juliet's stumbling. Your letter
and the ride through the wind, and perhaps, too,
the feeling that every day I am improving in

health and weight, made me feel more buoyant than I have felt for a long time.

November 23rd, Sunday

MARIA and I walked up to the parish church at Richard's castle to-day where Mr. Landon officiates. It is about a mile and a half from the Moor across the fields to Batchcott, and then up such a muddy lane to the top of the hill on which this picturesque little church stands. Can you imagine a greater shame than that of some supposed improver who plastered over the brown stone of which the church is built and from which the plaster is falling off in places? The stone tracery of the windows has not been desecrated, so that you can see and admire the rudely carved piercings. The tower, or campanile, is removed from the main body of the church some two or three yards and stands in front commanding the eminence and facing the east. Through the chancel is the entrance nearest the tower. It is built in the old style, and is at least one third the length of the church, being divided from the nave by an arch. It contains, merely, the communion table, under the eastern window, and the rails which surround it, as in our chancels.

Around the walls are the painted escutcheons of the Salways, and tablets to their memory adorn not only the walls, but are inserted in the marble floor. Entering the nave you advance several yards before you reach the reading-desk and pulpit, to the right of which is the only transept which contains the Salway pew, a great oaken stall with an oaken canopy covering this great square seat. We read the service out of immense prayer-books as large as the Mayor's and Aldermen's at Ludlow. Opposite us on the arch separating the nave from the chancel hung the painted escutcheons of the Salways in a black frame. Some barbarous innovator has plastered the interior of the church as well as the outside, and then whitewashed it. Charles Landon says that before they plastered the roof it was necessary to keep an umbrella open in rainy weather, for you could see the tiles through the rafters of the open roof.

At one side of the west window is a little oaken gallery where the children of the parish school sit, trained by the schoolmaster to assist in the singing. And such singing as it is! The schoolmaster leads and vainly endeavors to drown the voices of two females who both endeavor to out-scream each other. This is difficult, as every one sings in unison, except, indeed, one rash man who occasionally puts in a bass note between the turns and quivers of the schoolmaster and the two women. They began the service with a hymn, and to the first psalm, the 113th of our prayer-book, they sang the Portuguese Hymn with the most perfect Methodist turns and twang. Of course the chants were read.

In the piercings of the windows are some pretty specimens of antique stained glass. The church is small and the congregation still smaller, scattered here and there. Altogether the church and parish are deserving of a better rector than Mr. Landon, who I think goes through the service very much as if he were ashamed of it. The old clerk keeps a quid of tobacco in his mouth, and after a very long A—men, he spits over towards the Bridges pew.

Monday, November 24th

LADY HARRIET CLIVE returned to Oakly Park last Saturday and called here on Thursday in state, that is, with four horses and postillions. Unfortunately Aunt Catherine and Maria were out, and though Shaw invited Lady "'Arriet" in to see me, she excused herself and merely left cards for us. Lady Harriet is a great personage. Everybody stands in awe of her. She is very tall and dignified and as frigid as the Arctic Ocean. Mr. Betton says she expects people to walk out of the room backwards. Consequently it beseemed us to return her call as soon as possible, and to-day we went to Oakly Park. A glorious day it has been, although its brightness has been dimmed, as Lady Harriet was not at home, nor were Miss Clive nor Miss Mary Clive. However, we had an opportunity of seeing something of the place. The house is nothing remarkable, being built of brick and about twice the size of this house, but the grounds are very fine. It is three miles from Ludlow, and all the way you drive through the estate and enter the village of Bromfield, a portion of Mr. Clive's property. The village is most lovely. Lady Harriet encourages the tenants to improve their grounds and to render their houses picturesque with vines. Near the lodge gates is the parish church situated upon a rising ground which runs down to a mill stream. It looks very old, the embattled tower being partly covered with ivy, and making altogether a perfect representation of the church in Gray's "Elegy." Within the churchyard repose the honest poor, the yeomen of Bromfield, while in the church are laid the bones of all the Clives.

The drive through the avenue is very fine. Magnificent oaks, the cedar of Lebanon, the Scotch pine, the yew, the pollard oak, poplars, all so effectively and yet so massively arranged, beautify the scene. The greatest curiosities of the place are enormous oaks said to be Druidical. I suppose nowhere in the world do you ever see oaks of such a size but in England. The park seems of great extent; as far as the eye could reach you saw these magnificent oaks and finely grouped trees. There is but one thing I miss that I expected to see, and that, the deer roaming about. The corn laws have forced the parks into grazing cattle in order not to waste so much valuable ground, so that, instead of the deer that I expected to see, cattle were grazing or basking in the sun; and most singular-looking cattle some of them were, being scotched and perfectly black except sometimes their faces were white.

Mr. Clive is a younger son of a former Earl of Powis. This estate is his and yields at least ten thousand a year. Lady Harriet derives her income from her brother, the Earl of Plymouth, and has about forty thousand pounds a year. Miss Clive is very accomplished and draws wonderfully well. I saw herself and her father at the Ludlow church Sunday before last. I think Miss Clive must be twenty-seven or eight, and though not handsome, she is tall, and has a fine, intelligent face.

The Bridges called Thursday. According to the Landons' description, Mrs. Bridges is Lady Harriet Clive on a small scale, in manner, of course. Her daughters appear afraid of her and speak in a low, subdued tone. I never expect to know anything of them.

I draw regularly now from after breakfast until lunch at one o'clock. After lunch I either go to walk or ride, or we drive somewhere. You can't imagine how I enjoy my painting lessons. We have taken but two and I meet with such success that I am encouraged to go on. I find one lesson a week quite sufficient. Mr. Gill always leaves as many drawings as we wish, to study. I am learning in addition his style of pencil, a bold style I have long wished for, and I find that I acquire it without difficulty.

No wonder the English are such proficients in drawing and sketching. You can imagine nothing more exquisite than this country. It reminds me a little of the scenery about Northampton, with the addition of beautiful foregrounds. As a general thing the Northampton views were fine in the distance and in backgrounds. Here nothing can be more lovely than the distantly cultivated hills rising one on top of another, while in almost any position you place yourself you have some picturesque and vine-covered cottage, and beautifully disposed shrubbery and foliage for a foreground. They say Miss Clive has made some very fine sketches in this neighborhood, so I was particularly anxious to get in at Oakly Park, for Aunt Catherine had promised to finesse to get a peep at them. There are some original pictures of great value at Oakly Park — several Claudes, a Velasquez, and a Snyders, all very fine; besides, I suppose, some good modern paintings. Lady Harriet always gives a ball the first week in January, and I shall certainly have a chance then.

The young people are getting quite excited here as Christmas approaches, for there is always one public ball in Ludlow at which Lady Harriet presides, called Lady Harriet's Assembly, and a Charity Subscription ball. Last year all the principal people in the neighborhood entertained, so this year they do not anticipate so much gayety. I have one comfort — it is considered particularly genteel to be pale and slender. Girls with stout figures and rosy cheeks are called milkmaid beauties. It is funny how Americans are imagined by people who

have always lived in the country to be quite an
outlandish-looking race. Charles Landon imagined
he should see something very odd and *outré*, and
Miss Myrick asked me if I could speak Indian. I
am fortunate at least in being pale, for they cannot
suspect me of being one of the aborigines. The
people dress better than I expected to see. The
ladies always wear low necks and short sleeves
every day at dinner, so that Ned Landon, when
he sees me dressed for dinner, always says that I
would be smart if I were in a low dress. It saves a
great number of dresses. An English girl requires a
merino dress flounced for the morning, for visiting
and walking, and a white muslin for dinner. They
know nothing of the elegant demi-toilette. Imagine
walking through this great hall, sitting in the great
cold dining-room without anything over my neck!
Mrs. Landon always appears at dinner in red satin.
Uncle Richard has been over to Henley (Sir Charles
Cuyler's) shooting, for two successive Thursdays,
and has been both times persuaded into dining, and
though the dining-room is larger and as cold as ours,
the five Miss Cuylers were always dressed in white
muslin dresses and blue sashes.

I should have told you about these shooting
parties. For example, Thursday, Sir Charles in-
vited Uncle Richard, Mr. Roche, and Colonel
Russell to go over and shoot with him and to dine.
In order to be punctually there at nine o'clock,
Uncle Richard had to start early at eight o'clock, as

Sir Charles is exceedingly punctual. All day long they were at work, even until night, stopping only for lunch. I do not remember how many head of game they shot yesterday, for it was cover shooting. On another occasion, when Uncle Richard went over, rabbits were the sport, a very favorite amusement here, and they shot one hundred and four. It seems very strange that when one gentleman invites another to shoot with him he does not divide the game among them, but keeps all for himself. After the day's sport, they returned to Henley where Uncle Richard's portmanteau and a comfortable dressing-room prepared him to meet the party at dinner. Only two of the Miss Cuylers appeared at dinner. Uncle Richard found the others in the drawing-room.

Out of all these young ladies, only one is good looking — Miss Constance — and she appears to be admired only for her hair. From all accounts there is very little beauty about here. Miss Mary Bridges is considered a decided beauty, yet we would never notice her in America. It seems to me that so far as I have seen the great want among the young ladies is in manner and style. A young lady offers her hand for you to shake as if it were a pump handle, and there is no art more important than shaking hands gracefully, for if two dozen people enter a room, each one is expected to go around and shake hands with each one of the two dozen they may find in the room, and though they may only

stay two minutes the same ceremony is scrupu-
lously performed again. Sometimes the Landons,
having bade us good-bye with such energetic shakes
that I feel as if I were putting my hand in a thumb-
screw, find more to say and keep on talking for so
long a time that it is necessary for them to shake
hands all around again. I have given Ned several
lessons, so that now he is careful not to squeeze my
hand again.

November 30th, Sunday

UNCLE RICHARD had a shooting party yesterday,
composed of Sir Charles Cuyler, a prosperous baronet; Mr. Charlton, the last of an old and decayed
family; Mr. Betton; and Mr. Landon, the shooting
parson. They all dined here, so I shall be able to
describe them. Mr. Charlton is a bachelor of about
sixty, and resides at one of the oldest and most
picturesque places you can imagine. We are to go
over it some day when Aunt Catherine is well.
Until then I shall defer any description of it. Mr.
Charlton was the second son and had quite a handsome fortune, which he betted away upon the turf
until he became so involved that he was arrested
on his way to his brother's funeral, to whose large
but encumbered estates he succeeded. He has been
obliged to sacrifice a portion of Ludford, although
he still retains the house and a portion of land, and
keeps but one servant in the house to wait on him,
but the stud of horses which he retains are well

provided with grooms. He is tall and very thin, of a pale complexion. His hair, which was once sandy, is now too gray to be of any decided color. Mr. Landon whispered, with his wicked wink, that it was a wig, but I doubt it, as his teeth are fine. He has altogether the air of a used-up man, once the elegant gallant, now fallen into the sere and yellow leaf. Sir Charles is short and stout, red face and white hair as becomes the father of thirteen children. He has a diffident manner and a sweet maidenly smile. Mr. Betton and Mr. Landon have already appeared upon the stage, so that you are quite acquainted with the *dramatis personæ* about to appear.

Scene I, Act I

The drawing-room, Mrs. Fay elegantly dressed, reclining upon a couch in consequence of lameness (produced by boils from which she has been confined to bed for some days). Mr. Fay stands before the fire, his hands under his coat-tails. Miss A. M. Fay in blue silk, sits modestly in the chimney corner. Miss Maria Fay is completing her toilette above. Steps are heard on the stairs. The door opens. Sir Charles Cuyler is announced. Then follow at intervals Mr. Landon, Mr. Charlton, and last, Mr. Betton. During the few moments preceding dinner the weather is discussed. Each one has successively exclaimed — "Very cowald day!" The door opens, Shaw announces dinner, Mrs. Fay is placed in her wheel chair to be wheeled into the dining-room. Sir Charles offers his arm to Miss Fay, Mr. Charlton to Miss A. M. Fay, and the scene changes to the dining-room. And here I drop the dramatic form.

Maria was seated between Sir Charles and Mr. Betton. On my right hand I had Mr. Landon, who is deaf in his left ear; and on my left, Mr. Charlton, who informed me that he was deaf in his right ear. Notwithstanding the prospect thus opened, I had a very pleasant time. They were all sociable and agreeable. Conundrums were introduced accidentally, and Sir Charles proved himself quite a proficient. Then that never-ending theme of poachers came up. I cannot imagine what English country gentlemen would do were there no poachers. Mention the word, and you set Mr. Betton off. He fights all his battles o'er again. He enlarges upon the villainy of poachers, upon the ingratitude of poachers, tells anecdotes about poachers, until you grow so nervous that you expect to see a poacher start up and seize the bird upon your plate. Naturally the conversation turns upon the day's sport, and you hear how that bird was winged; how another was tailered; how many cock pheasants were shot; how many hen pheasants were deprived of life; how many woodcock were put up; how many partridges flew out of one cover; how many rabbits were killed; who shot well; who shot badly; who missed fire; whose cock pheasant fell with his tail up; whose hen pheasant with her tail down; who shot on this side the dingle, who on the other, and so forth, and so forth, and so on. Then the meet of the previous day takes its turn — who fell in leaping over this hurdle, who in taking that hedge, who fell on his feet, who on his head, where the fox was found, and where killed, and how the sport was spoiled on account of the frost, and how cold it was, and how cold it is, and how cold it is going to be, and how unusual it is, such weather unheard of at this season, and how fine the autumn has been — and then you rise from the table and you leave the gentlemen to discuss, more at large, poaching, shooting, hunting, and the cold, unrestrained by female society. After a while they come into the drawing-room and the card-table is taken out, the gentlemen cut to play and the rest look on. They are not a very intellectual set, these country gentlemen, but they are very sociable and pleasant. I like Sir Charles very much. He is very unassuming and affable, and has been exceedingly polite to Uncle Richard. He is cousin to Mrs. Robert Leroy, of New York. He came up to talk to me and began immediately about the balls. He says Lady Harriet's ball does not come off until January.

I am sure you would like to know what we had for dinner. Hare soup first, of course; then boiled cod and oyster sauce; next, boiled chickens and an American ham; meat balls and cutlets, and vegetables; then venison and partridges; after that, mince pies and some sort of trifle; and last, the dessert — delicious grapes and apples and pears, and other little things. I wish my mother could see the English poultry. There is nothing like them. The ducks are finer than anything I ever tasted. Every day almost since I have been here we have had some kind of game or another, and the hothouse furnishes delicious grapes. Yesterday they killed twenty-three pheasants and twenty-five rabbits. I felt dreadfully at having the pheasants shot, for they look so beautiful running out of the covers. They are almost as tame as chickens.

Aunt Catherine is still suffering much from her lameness, and is confined to her sofa.

Tuesday, December 2nd

YESTERDAY made an addition to our acquaintance. Captain Russell called. He is the son of the late General Russell, and lives with his mother and sisters in a large house very near to us. They have recently lost their father, and they have only just begun to make visits. The Captain informed us that his sisters would call very soon. The Russells are cousins to the Lowells of Boston, and have quite a number of American relatives. It seemed that, as their father had been dead eight months, they might have laid aside the usual ceremony and called sooner. Judging, however, from the width of the black edge upon the Captain's card, their mourning is very deep. The young ladies are decided belles, and one is said to be very handsome. The Captain called very soon after lunch, at which time Aunt Catherine was just getting up. Maria was not dressed, so that I, being in my blue and red silk, and black silk basquine, was the only person ready to go down and receive him. Accordingly, I was sent off. Shaw, who is perfectly *au fait* and considerate, opened the door and announced me, saving me the necessity of introducing myself. I found Captain Russell very pleasant during the half-hour we waited for Aunt Catherine's appearance. He is quite an elegant, with his black moustache, although I do not admire an Englishman with black hair.

To-day Kitty and I went out riding after lunch, with Mr. Charlton accidentally our cavalier. Ah, if you could have seen Mr. Charlton's horse! Such a beauty! and one of those long racers you see in pictures. At Batchcott, Mr. Ogle joined us on the most wretched-looking animal. A division of the party ensued, when Mr. Charlton fell to my lot, or rather, I took him in preference a thousand times to the young and good-looking but rough Mr. Ogle. We went with Mr. Charlton to Orleton to buy a pig. I found him (Mr. Charlton) very pleasant and very eccentric — very much such a person in appearance, though more polished in manner, as Mr. Edward Clark, of Northampton. I am afraid, however, that by means of this ride I have got out of Ned Landon's good graces, for I promised to go to walk with him. I was in the unfortunate position that all persons are who wish to please everybody.

I wish you would tell John that Sunday after church we went up in the organ loft and there I procured a list of the stops and that I am only waiting for his letter to send them. I write so fully to you that I must keep something for him. Do not think that I am wrapped up in myself and my own amusements. In reading over what I have written, it seems to me that I speak only of myself and what surrounds me. It is not because I am becoming forgetful of you all at home, but, on the contrary, because I wish to make my pleasures as much yours as possible, and to tell you everything that will interest you; in fact, to do as I would be done by — remember that. Be pleased to observe that you cannot tell me anything too trivial.

HISTORY OF THE CASTLE

Ludlow contains several objects of interest, not the least important of which is the castle, where kings have dwelt, whose crumbling walls have often echoed to the voice of mirth and with the din of war.

Ludlow, being so near the Welsh borders, was drawn into the strifes of those feudal days and thus the castle became the scene of some notable events. The beadle, whose limited information was not equal to our close questioning, recommended to me a book from which I hope to gather some facts which I think will interest you.

The noble ruins of the castle are situated on an eminence, on the banks of the Teme and command the whole town. The castle was begun by Roger de Montgomery, a kinsman of the Conqueror, but the only part which he completed was the dongeon or keep in 1090. Roger de Montgomery and his sons entered zealously into the troubles caused by the contest between the sons of William the Conqueror. Indeed, of such a meddling disposition were these Montgomerys that Roger's second son, who succeeded to the titles and estate after the death of his elder brother, was convicted of treason against his King, Henry the First, and banished the kingdom, and his confiscated estates given to Joce or Gosto, who took the name Dinan from the town and castle of that name. This Joce de Dinan finished the Castle of Ludlow and fortified himself against his enemies, among whom were Hugh de Mortimer of Wigmore and Hugh de Lacy, who laid claim to this goodly castle, and would have gained possession of it, had not Dinan been so fortunate as to have a daughter, Henvyse, by name, as brave as she was fair, who incited her lover, Fulke Fitz-Warine, to draw his maiden sword in her father's defence, and thus not only saved his life, but captured his enemy, Sir Walter de Lacy, and his companion, Arnold de Lisle, whom he immediately confined in the Tower, called Pendover. Love, however, who defies bolts and bars, pierced the heart of the maiden named Marion dela Bruere with love of the valiant knight, Arnold de Lisle, and she faithlessly assisted in the escape of Sir Walter and her lover. There now succeeded renewed strife, for Sir Walter set to work at once to revenge himself upon Joce, but peace being finally restored, the fair Henvyse conferred her hand upon Fulke, which event gave rise to great festivities and ended in a wedding tour accompanied by Joce, on which occasion Marion wrote to her lover Arnold, who not only came himself, but brought with him Sir Walter and a number of armed men.

By means of the ladder with which Marion had assisted the ascent of Arnold, Sir Walter effected his entrance into the castle, put to death the guard, and then sallied into the town carrying death and destruction with him. When Marion discovered what she had done, she slew her lover and then jumped out of the window. This, however, did not mend the matter, for Joce de Dinan, though he fought most valiantly, never recovered his castle, but was finally taken prisoner by the ruthless Sir Walter de Lacy. Though King John wrested the castle from him, it was finally restored and remained an important post during the border troubles. After many years it came into the possession of the Mortimers of Wigmore, so renowned for their pretensions to the English throne through the

marriage of Edmund de Mortimer with Phillipa
Plantagenet, daughter and heiress of Lionel, Duke
of Clarence.

Richard, Duke of York, and a descendant by
this marriage of Edward the Third, made Ludlow
his headquarters, and, though he was finally slain,
his son Edward, Earl of March, continued the
contest and died leaving his son Edward to gain
the long-desired kingdom and to ascend the throne
as Edward the Fourth.

In reward for all the disasters which this long and
painful contest had caused the town of Ludlow, the
King granted it an important charter. It was to
this castle that Edward sent his infant sons,
Edward, newly created Prince of Wales, and his
young brother, and here they remained. After the
death of their father, they were removed to London
by Richard the Third, to perish in the Tower.
Henry the Seventh, following the example of
Edward, sent his son Arthur to Ludlow, and often
came here himself, but the untimely death of his
son cut off his sympathies with the border, and
thus Ludlow Castle was converted into the seat of
a regular court of jurisdiction for governing Wales.

Many distinguished men, both prelates and lay-
men, dwelt here as Lord Presidents, none of whom
were so renowned as Sir Henry Sidney. It was upon
the occasion of the visit of King Charles the First
to the castle that Milton wrote his "Comus." It
was enacted in the presence of the King by the sons

and daughters of the then Lord President, the Earl of Bridgewater.

During the Civil War Ludlow Castle fell into the hands of the Puritans, an event to be forever deplored had it not been the means of affording an asylum to Butler, who was appointed Secretary to the Governor, Richard Lord Vaughan, and the precise place is shown where he is said to have written his "Hudibras." Ludlow Castle continued to be governed by the Presidents until the court for the government of Wales was dissolved by act of Parliament in 1689. One of these Governors was so severe a man that the following distich was written upon him:

"Here lies Sir John Bridgeman and clad in his clay,
God said to the Devil, 'Sirrah, take him away.'"

IV

My dear H——:

The long passage of the steamer kept me on the *qui vive* for two days. I could not draw before eleven o'clock, in anticipation of the arrival of the postbag, and I could do nothing afterwards from disappointment. Yesterday eleven o'clock came, and Mrs. Mound did not make her appearance, so I put on my bonnet and shawl to run down to the lodge after the postbag, providing myself at the same time with the key. I had not proceeded far before I met Mrs. Mound with the bag, and it did not take a minute to open it and find myself possessor of your letter. I ran upstairs to Aunt Catherine's room, threw the bag and its contents into her lap, and was soon in the midst of your letter, reading it out, of course, for the benefit of herself and Maria. Later in the day, Aunt Catherine requested a second reading, for she has one of those delightful dispositions which takes a delight in all that concerns her friends.

I am shocked at the loss of my letter, for it was sent at the same time as Maria's was, who was far less anxious to get hers off. It had been a subject of grumbling with me for ten days, that I feared

my letter would not be in time for the steamer.
Besides, it had been a great pleasure to me to
write, and some of my most agreeable hours were
spent sitting on the floor of the cabin and writing
on my lap. Send to Mary White [1] and get her to
lend you Maria's letter, for I would not for the
world that you should lose the acquaintance of
the charming Colomb. I am happy that the one
you did receive gave you pleasure. It is my greatest happiness to describe everything as graphically
as possible, that you may enjoy with me. I am
only too happy if I succeed. I could not be sufficiently delighted that you are all so well. Tell
Clara [2] that I have read her letter over a great many
times, and that I have not yet seen a little girl like
her. Another time I shall expect to hear from Susy
and Willie. [3]

I have wished many times the last few days that
you were here to enjoy the delicious weather that
we have had. The cold of last week has subsided
into the most lovely springlike air, and I have
enjoyed life and the pleasures of nature to a degree
that I feel as if I should like to live forever. Willie
(Fay) and I have had the most charming rides for
the last three days. We prefer, as a general thing, to
go through Richard's castle to Orleton, which gives
us a ride of five or six miles. You should see us receive the salutations of the cottagers — the gracious

[1] Mrs. Howard Elliott.   [2] The author's sister.
[3] Her sister and brother.

bow we give to the elders, and the smile we bestow upon the little ones. Indeed, I do not flatter myself, I am sure, when I say that no lady of the Manor could find fault with the style in which I confer these favors. Willie, dear little cavalier, confirms me in this opinion, and compliments me upon the smile I give the boys when they pull their forelocks and the little girls as they curtsey.

To-day has been more lovely than any that have preceded it. Kitty and Miss Dodd and myself went up to church at Richard's castle, and then after service Ned Landon took us to see the Bony Well below the church, so called because every March and April bones are found in it like those of frogs. Whence they come nobody has been able to discover. Above it, on the hill, are the remains of the castle, consisting merely of a part of an arch and wall. We came home across Hanway Common, from which the view is so exquisite that I am sure Milton must have stood here before he wrote —

"Straight mine eye hath caught new pleasures
While the landscape round it measures."
("L'Allegro.")

Indeed, the world around me has been so beautiful and peaceful, and the sky so mild and serene, that I could hardly realize that I could be so near the terrible events happening in Paris.

You will have some idea of how moderate the climate is when I tell you that vines in bloom cover many of the cottages and that roses can be picked any day in the garden. Indeed, the ground seldom freezes so that the farmers cannot plough. It would remind me of the Savannah climate were it not that the sun has so little power. We get up every morning at eight o'clock and we have the advantage of the sunrise. About noon his glorious majesty, if he be not enveloped in a cloudy veil — for a clear sunrise is not always auspicious of a clear day — does not appear more than thirty or forty degrees above the horizon. By four o'clock he has disappeared and left hardly a ray behind — perhaps to new trick his dreams for another beautiful day. No wonder, then, surrounded thus within doors and without by sources of so much enjoyment, that I found to-day (Monday) on my visit to Ludlow and a grocery shop that I weighed one hundred and fourteen without my clogs. I have gained ten pounds at least since I have been here — about two pounds a week, and now I am within six pounds of one hundred and twenty.

Wednesday, the 10th

THUS far the week has passed very quietly. We have seen the Landons as usual every day. Why I am not talked out with them I cannot imagine. They have always lived here, except Charles, who comes from Devonshire and thinks it superior to the rest of the world. They care only for the narrow sphere in which they live and are utterly without aspirations, provided the hounds meet on the appointed day and Henry's pony is in good order, and Ned gets a mount, Mr. Landon an occasional shooting and his dinner, and Mrs. Landon and Janet their walk after lunch. Europe might be convulsed with revolutions, Asia and Africa submerged, and the Western continent burnt up, for all they would care. It surprises me to see people live such a life of inaction — without a thought or a wish beyond to-morrow and not.an aspiration for any change or anything new; contented to come over here every day and discuss the merits and demerits of the various young ladies of the neighborhood. For my part, I always refer to these interesting subjects with renewed zest. They are not less wearying to me than to the Landons. Every day I ask the same questions and elicit the same replies. George, the eldest son, is expected on Monday from Oxford, where he is studying for a living — for theological students in England have only that in view. He is devoted to cricket and boating, so there will be some new themes for conversation. Never again shall I complain of the want of gallantry of Americans, for you would be shocked to hear these young men talk of young ladies. I tell them it destroys all pleasure in their conversation, because I expect to share the same fate. I have had several quarrels with Ned on the subject and think he is a little improved.

I had hoped to be able this time to tell you about the castle and Mr. Charlton's house, but Aunt

Catherine still continues to suffer so much with her lameness as to be obliged to walk with crutches, and we have been compelled to put off the visit to the castle and the lunch at Mr. Clarke's. I hope by the time Richard (Fay) comes, which will be the day before Christmas, that she will be well enough to go about with us. I find no want of amusement in my pursuits, and our walks and rides and the Landons' visits. Indeed, nothing seems tame, nor do I tire of seeing the same thing over and over again, but unfortunately, although the impressions I receive are always varied, my mode of giving expression to them is limited, and I fear my letters would soon become tiresome.

There is but one advantage of which I have not availed myself since I have been here and with which you may reproach me, and that is the sources of improvement which the library affords. With what delight would some lover of ancient lore find himself within reach of these rare editions of old authors, but I, Goth that I am, because they want a painted border, have not an odor of sheep-skin, and are printed in plain clear type instead of illegible written characters, find no interest in them. Fancy any one enjoying Pontoppidan's "History of Norway" or Pocock's "Travels." Such names would be enough to frighten one in the very beginning, and then I doubt whether I should be more interesting when I returned if I had gone through all the classics and worked on philosophy, the-

ology, and physics, with which the library abounds.
You might imagine that a book entitled Middle-
ton's "Inquiry" would have tempted me to look
beyond the lettering on the back, but alas! the
title-page told the story that put at once an end to
my interest. The "Inquiry" concerned only "The
Miraculous Powers of the Christian Church" during certain centuries. Possessing as I do the reputation of being romantic, it may seem equally strange
that I have not been interested in "The Memoir of
an Unfortunate Young Nobleman Return'd from
a Thirteen Years' Slavery in America where he had
been sent with the Wicked Contrivances of his
Cruel Uncle — A Story Founded on Truth and address'd equally to the Head and the Heart." Indeed, far from having read the four volumes of
"Pamela," or "Clarissa," or "Sir Charles Grand-
ison," I have not even availed myself of "A Collection of the Moral and Instructive Maxims,
Cautions, and Reflections Contain'd in the Histories" of these interesting persons. I confess I do
not sympathize with "The Female Quixote," in her
imitation of those heroines of antiquity — Par-
isatis, Clelia, Mandana, nor do I approve of the
manner in which she treated her lovers because they
were not like the divine Oroondates or the constant
Artaxerxes. These, to be sure, are not the only
novels. There are others by Richardson and Field-
ing and Smollett, but they are not to be mentioned, much less thought of — why! Miss Dodd

would not so much as express an opinion of them in English. In French only could she find language to apply to such a subject. If others desecrate English in such a way, Doddy is determined not to countenance it. As a general thing, we depend upon Mr. Partridge's circulating library for our reading. Early imbued, as you know, with Sir Anthony Absolute's prejudices, I felt in plucking the fruit from this evergreen tree of diabolical knowledge almost as guilty as Eve, but I have fortunately experienced none of the ill effects to be anticipated. Having waded through several three volume novels, I am certainly none the wiser and I trust not the worse. Mr. Partridge at least affords the pleasure of following "Leonard" (Bulwer) in his career.

Fancy my being in possession the first of the month of what you are dying to know, and yet not having the means to tell you. The British steamer brings us every week the weekly "Herald" and other American papers, and Sunday's mail the "Weekly Dispatch" and "Bell's Life." Ah! now I imagine you start at a familiar name. You remember, as I do, that every fast young man in novels is represented stretched back in a chair, his feet on the fender, a cigar in his mouth, the walls of his room hung with pictures of opera dancers and race-horses, and "Bell's Life" in his hands, and if your imagination be as limited as mine, you will wonder whether it were a book, a pamphlet, or an almanac, and in what the interest consisted; but the simple fact will never have presented itself to you that "Bell's Life" in London is a weekly sporting paper. I hope and trust that you are as ignorant as I was, for the law does not provide that useless information be not included in the half-ounce. If I have acquired a virtue since I have been abroad, it is that I weigh well what I write. Every sentence ought to have its due weight, for when tried in the balance four sheets and the envelope will not admit of even dust being added. I hope on the other side of the Atlantic the scales are equally just and that you never have to pay double postage.

Tuesday, 16*th*

Sir William Rouse-Boughton and the two Misses Rouse-Boughton, and their *dame de compagnie*, called to-day. Unfortunately, I was out riding with Willie, but as we came up the short avenue we met them where the road is so narrow that they stopped to let us pass, so that if I had not been near-sighted I should have had a good view of them. Sir William Boughton is the owner of Downton Hall and during his life the magnificent estate of Downton Castle, which at his death goes to his second son, left him by his maternal grandmother. Downton Hall and Downton Castle are eight miles apart, and Sir William owns all the intermediate land, and has, they say, upon it

£200,000 worth of timber that ought to be felled. He begged Aunt Catherine to name a day to dine there, but she did not accept his very urgent and polite invitation until Richard's return, as it does not agree with Uncle Richard to dine out. The Teme runs through the grounds near Downton Castle, and the cliffs through which it passes are in places a hundred feet high. We planned several expeditions there, but Aunt Catherine's illness put an end to them.

In my next letter I hope to be able to make up for this uninteresting one. Christmas is to be celebrated in true English style. We shall go to Downton and probably to the castle and Mr. Charlton's, and I shall have, I hope, much to describe. I cannot help longing that I could pass Christmas at home with you all. I constantly think of how pleasantly we were engaged last year at this time preparing the children's dolls, and how little I thought that this year I should be writing of Christmas at the Moor Park, a place I never even dreamed of.

. . . .

I have almost forgotten to tell you that poor Mr. Gill is in such ill health that he has been obliged to give up our painting lessons in favor of a younger brother, whom, however, we like better. His paintings and drawings are better finished, and I think his method is better. He takes the same liberty with his *h*'s, and always says, as it may happen — "Sure yes," or "Sure no."

The first part of my letter will make you think that everybody has falsified the English climate. November was a remarkably fine month. Indeed, the oldest inhabitant says such a one has hardly ever been known, but December is determined to give us a specimen of an English winter. For a week almost we have not seen the sun, and we have constant fogs. As the Landons would say, the walking is "beastly." Tell Willie that Ned Landon brought me a fox's brush, but it had such a "nasty stinking smell" that he took it to cure and I shall bring it home for him. Don't think that I am getting vulgar. That is an aristocratic mode of expressing your opinion of a bad smell.

V

I SEIZE the first leisure moment of this week to begin one of my interminable epistles. Your letter did not reach me until Sunday, it having probably remained in Uncle Henry's[1] pocket too long. The familiar "H" upon the seal informed me, before I looked at the postmark, that you were in New York. You can imagine that I was not a little astonished and delighted, besides, that you should have a chance of enjoying yourself. Lively blushes, as Maria would say, cover my cheeks while I acknowledge and accept the compliments lavished upon my humble efforts at letter-writing.

But now it is time that I should begin to tell you what I have been doing since I last wrote. The date at the top of this page will tell you that Christmas is over and gone. I feel that during all my life I shall look back upon these few last days as a period of unalloyed enjoyment — unalloyed I should not have said, for with every pleasure was mingled a regret that you and my mother and the children were not sharing it. If, however, I may be permitted to use the Dick Swiveller style, I should say that it will always be a "green spot in memory's desert." The week began with a most pleas-

[1] Her uncle, Mr. Henry Hills.

ant surprise — Richard, whom we did not expect
until Wednesday, walked in while we were at
breakfast accompanied by his friend Frank Peabody — Richard from Bonn, and Frank from the
École des Beaux Arts, Paris. The joyful greeting
may be better imagined than described. Suffice it
to say that Richard was unchanged in appearance,
except that his face was fuller and his moustache
more formidable. Frank Peabody is just the person
to enter heart and soul into a frolic. Small in
person, nimble as a mouse, full of fun and humor,
you can imagine that with the addition of our
elegant Richard and his charming friend the preparations for the Christmas amusements began
with renewed vigor. Visions of kisses under the
mistletoe were called up. Frank Peabody and
Richard were willing to climb to inaccessible
heights to obtain it, until Uncle Richard damped
their ardor by ordering the gardener to perform
that important duty. George Landon, the Oxon-
ian, proposed charades, and came on Wednesday
evening to consult about the words. We found to
our surprise that in certain characters he was admirable. As Miss Dobbs, the bashful old maid, and
the footman, he acted to the life; at the same time,
Frank Peabody developed powers which threat-
ened to undo all the restraints I had been forced to
adopt in order to keep the hooks on my dresses.
So the time passed, not, however, without other
pleasures than those of anticipation. Richard and

I took some charming rides and danced and sang —
that is, Maria and Richard sang and I was only too
happy to listen.

The children could not restrain their impatience
for Christmas Eve to arrive, when stockings were
to be hung at every door, to provide for which
Santa Claus had been some time ready. At last it
came, and with it the carols. Some boys chanted
under the windows the story of the Saviour's
birth, the church bells rang, and all told of the
coming day. After a frolicsome evening, we went
upstairs, each one to act the part of Santa Claus —
and what with running about from door to door,
and then listening at our own until our stockings
were filled, we did not get to bed until one o'clock.
And notwithstanding the additional inducements
held out to us to get up before the first bell, I must
confess we overslept ourselves on Christmas morning.

However, at last aroused, the stockings were
quickly seized. Mine opened, behold! a little velvet
boot filled with chocolates, a pair of scales, and a
barrel filled in a like manner from Frank Peabody,
a Berlin bracelet, and half a ream of this paper
from Richard, a Pyrenese bracelet from Aunt
Catherine, "Paul and Virginia" from Kitty, a
papetrie from Lily, and shawl-pin from Maria.
Maria draws out her presents. She is the possessor
of a bass viol and a whirl-a-gig filled with bonbons
from Frank, music from Richard, a Pyrenese

bracelet from Aunt Catherine, and little knick-knacks from the children. Kitty displays a beautiful pair of sabots, and she is not expected to fill them with peas and to walk in them, for they are well stocked with delicious bonbons. Each one has something pretty to show when we meet. "Merry Christmas!" passes from mouth to mouth. Every one is happy, every one joyful. The little boys sing again the Christmas carols. They tell us in our mirth to remember that Christ is born this day. Baskets of holly are brought in with which to deck the house. Eager hands seize the magnificent mistletoe bough. Richard obtains kisses without trouble, but Frank has to struggle for them, which, of course, makes them all the more valuable. At last it is hung between the folding doors. Maria and I start off for church and leave the rest to dress the house, and when we return we find the holly tastefully disposed everywhere, and preparations going on for the charades. Kitty and Frank are painting little English and American flags with which to adorn the mantelpiece, and then Richard and I go off on horseback to get some wool for a wig. The children dine with us at five o'clock. We have the English Christmas dishes, boiled turkey and plum pudding; and game from America — canvasback ducks, quail and partridges, six brace of each having been sent by Mr. Codman and Rodman from Boston.

At half-past eight o'clock the Landons make

their appearance. Each makes some significant remark about the mistletoe, and as Charles asks me
to dance he displays his intentions so evidently
that I elude his grasp, which, however, does not
prevent my being subjected to the ceremony later
in the evening.

After a little dance, preparations began for the
charades. A table was brought in, covered with
packages of documents, and in marches Uncle
Richard in gown and wig followed by Richard and
George Landon as lawyers, preceded by the sheriff,
Frank Peabody, who in the funniest manner cries
— "Oyez! Oyez!" and the rest of the formula. The
judge opens the case. It is a breach of promise case.
Absurd letters are read, and the facts stated.
Meantime, Frank, out of sight of the judge, keeps
the audience in a roar of laughter by an absurd
pantomime. The scene ended. The company discovered the first word to be "Court." Scene second
opens with Uncle Richard walking up and down in
the American naval costume. They are about to
enact an incident which occurred last year on
board the Constitution. Frank Peabody runs
about in a sailor's dress, pulling ropes, and giving
as much as possible the appearance of the deck of a
vessel. Presently the suite of the Court of Naples
is announced. The captain shows them the ship,
explains various sails and ropes, which the courtiers
examine with their glasses to their eyes. They go
peering about as if they were walking on eggs.

Suddenly one of them disappears, and Frank as a
sailor comes swaggering up, touches his cap, and
with the true Yankee twang says — "Cap'n, one
of them ere kings has fallen down the ventilator."
Every one exclaims — "Ship"; and "Courtship"
is the whole word. In the whole word, Aunt
Catherine and Frank act. Frank is seated in the
most awkward and uncomfortable position, does
not know what to do with himself, when the door
opens and Miss Fanny Bloomer is announced.
Miss Fanny's costume is quite effective. A short
dress, full pantalettes, etc. She runs up to Frank,
seizes his hand, and seats herself beside him; while
he, poor fellow, seems frightened to death and
tries to get away — but to no purpose, for Miss
Fanny does not relax her hold, but pours out her
love. She tells him that the trammels Society has
imposed have forced her to bury in her bosom a
never-dying love for him, but now that the world
has awakened to the wrongs of woman and burst
these restraints, she avails herself of the new privileges of her sex and offers him her hand and heart.
This throws the shy young man into such a state
that he jumps up frantically from his seat, and the
adroit Miss Fanny, taking advantage of his dis-
traction, gets him under the mistletoe and is in the
act of kissing him when his cries bring his servant
to his rescue, who carries him off in his arms. The
whole scene is admirably acted. Nothing could be
better than Aunt Catherine as Miss Bloomer, and

Frank Peabody acted his part admirably. All we wanted was a larger audience.

After the charades we had a little more dancing, and the Landons took their leave. Fatigued by our exertions, we seated ourselves around the fire. Only one lamp was left burning, and, as the witching hour approached, Frank Peabody proposed to tell ghost stories. Uncle Richard told us of a murder which occurred in our room, which was so interesting that I must tell you of it. The grandfather of the present proprietor had a beautiful niece who lived with him and with whom his son was passionately in love. Tradition says that she was beautiful, and her portrait which hangs in the hall represents a lovely girl of eighteen. It appears that she did not return the love of her cousin, for she was engaged to a young curate who lived in Elton. One afternoon, as was his custom, the young clergyman came over to see his lady-love on horseback. Unsuspicious of evil, they walked in the garden in probably a very lover-like manner, not knowing that they were watched by the jealous cousin.

At the usual hour they separated at the door which leads from the garden, and the young lady went to her room. Time passed, and she did not come downstairs, and at last a servant was sent to see why she did not come down — when she was found lying on the floor, dead and weltering in her own blood. In the meantime the cousin had hurried to the stable and saddled a horse, and was seen to ride frantically off. In about two hours he returned and went to his room, and when the door was forced open he was found hanging by the neck. At the same time the young clergyman was discovered on the road, if not dead, past cure and insensible. The cousin's room was opposite ours, or, rather, the one occupied by the young lady. You can imagine that such an event created a great sensation, and even now it is looked upon as such a stain upon the family history that, when her portrait is shown, you are told that she died young, and you cannot help looking at the beautiful face again and again. There is a fascination about it from which you cannot get away.

December 29*th*

FRANK PEABODY left to-day, to our regret. Mr. Clive called yesterday, and Aunt Catherine promised that we should dine at Oakly Park, but the day is not yet fixed. The door of the carriage has been broken off by the carelessness of a servant, so that we have not yet returned the Boughtons' visit. The ball comes off on Friday. It takes place in a large hall at Ludlow, and Lady Harriet is patroness, and the Earl of Powis steward. Among Mr. Clive's great connections is his sister, the Duchess of Northumberland, who was governess to the Queen. The Clives are not going to give a ball this year as usual.

I received your letter, as unexpected as delightful, the day after Christmas.

You ask me about my wardrobe. I find it quite suitable. The greatest objection is that everything is too tight for me. I wore my white muslin on Christmas Eve, and though I put in a new back it burst out in every direction. The insertion down the entire length of the shoulders burst asunder, the hem down one side gave way, and the dancing caused destruction of what otherwise would have held together. So you can imagine that it is in a rather dilapidated condition. My habit does quite well as long as the roads are so muddy. Richard and Frank Peabody liked my hat particularly. Later in the season I should like a new habit, although how to get it made is the question. You would be amused to see me walk about Ludlow in my habit. We put our horses up at the Angel Inn, and, of course, I am free to go about and shop, or do what I wish. Yesterday Richard, Willie, and I went into town, and, as I was sitting on the pony opposite the Angel Inn until Richard had his horse put up, an old gentleman with such a red face and such a sweet smile came up to speak to me. His face was familiar to me, but it was not for some moments that I could recall his name, when I hastened to repair my awkwardness by inquiring after Lady Cuyler, for it was sweet Sir Charles.

You can imagine what pleasure it is to ride about with Richard. He is not less grave than he used to be, but I think he endeavors more to make himself generally agreeable, and he is much improved in every respect. He is remarkably elegant in appearance. The repose of his manner accords perfectly to my taste with his fine classical face. I think his mother would like to have him gay like other young men, but I do not think it would suit him.

January 1st

HAPPY NEW YEAR! The carollers have again been to sing for us to tell us that the New Year has come. The church bells rang the Old Year out and the New Year in. We go to-day to dine at Oakly Park. It was a most delicate attention on the part of Lady Harriet, for as the ball takes place to-morrow she wished to know us before that great event. They are exceedingly cordial. Uncle Richard has laid aside his invariable rule and has accepted. The nobility have been so far more polite than the gentry. I shall wear my white barège this evening and my tarleton to-morrow evening. We dine next Wednesday at Mrs. Myrick's, and on Monday we go to pay our first visit at Downton Hall, and I suppose we shall soon dine there.

VI

MY DEAR H——:

The pleasures of last evening deserve an extra
letter. I had intended writing to Cousin Margaret
an account of the dinner, but I would not care to
give her so minute a description of it as you would
like; and, as I know your gratification and my
mother's would be so great, I hasten by entering
into every particular to afford you at least a portion of the pleasure that I enjoyed. You can
imagine that having so constantly heard of Lady
Harriet's being formal and stiff, I should dread my
first dinner there, particularly, and therefore it
was with a beating heart I found myself at the hall
door. Two footmen in red plush breeches and blue
coats and silver buttons, and the groom of the
chambers in black, received us in the vestibule,
where we took off our cloaks. The dignitary in
black preceded us through the hall and throwing
open the door announced us as Mr. and Mrs. Fay,
and the Miss Fays, and Mr. Fay. We found ourselves in a large and beautiful library, and an
elegant circle of ladies and gentlemen rose to meet
us. Lady Harriet received us with great dignity,
and though no one was introduced every one spoke
to us. It was not until the end of the evening that

we knew who composed the party, and I will tell
you here, that you may know in what distinguished
company we dined. When dinner was announced,
Mr. Clive rose and offered his arm to the Dowager
Countess of Powis, a fine-looking woman very
much in Aunt Margaret's[1] style, and very beautifully dressed in a French gray damask, very much
like one Aunt Margaret had. On her neck was a
pearl necklace and on a pendant attached to it
was a countess's coronet in diamonds with a cipher
underneath. Of course her rank gave her precedence over Aunt Catherine, whom Lady Harriet
requested Mr. Robert Clive, the heir of the house,
to take in to dinner. Aunt Catherine looked more
elegant than either Lady Powis or Lady Harriet.
Her commanding height gave great effect to her
beautiful Parisian dress. Then Uncle Richard followed with Lady Lucy Herbert, a very pretty girl
with an exquisite figure and beautifully dressed.
She preceded Lady Harriet Herbert and a Mr.
Clive. Lady Harriet Herbert is a lively, charming
creature, full of fun and frolic. Her figure was most
beautiful, and they were both as pale as American
girls. They are daughters of the Countess of
Powis and sisters of the Earl of Powis. After these,
Maria followed with the Honorable Mr. Herbert.
She looked exceedingly well and was very prettily
dressed. Lady Harriet requested the Honorable
William Herbert to take me in; then Miss Clive

[1] Mrs. Henry Hills, of New York.

and Mr. Longworth, the Vicar of Bromfield; and Richard and Miss Mary Clive followed; and finally Lady Harriet and the Earl of Powis, who is a bachelor of about thirty-five. Without being handsome Lady Harriet is a fine aristocratic-looking woman, and not half so formidable as she has been represented.

We found ourselves in a large dining-room hung with pictures, among which preëminent was the portrait of the great Robert Clive, grandfather of the present possessor. Seated at a beautiful table, we found ourselves in a family circle, which made the compliment all the greater. At the head of the table, which was long and broad, sat Mr. Clive and Lady Powis. On his right was Aunt Catherine, and next to her Mr. Robert Clive; then Maria and Mr. Herbert; next Mr. Clive and Lady Harriet Herbert; then Richard and Miss Mary Clive. At the foot of the table were the Earl of Powis and Lady Harriet. Uncle Richard was on Lady Harriet's left, and beside him Lady Lucy Herbert; then a shy young man whose name I do not know; then a young son of the Clives, the Honorable William and myself. Miss Clive sat next to me, and Mr. Longworth on the left of the Countess. Thus you have us seated at the table after grace by Mr. Longworth.

Now I must describe the arrangement of the hospitable board. In the centre of the table was a gilt plateau on which stood two immense candelabras with ornaments of china figures. At each end of the table were two candelabras on stands similar though smaller than the plateau. The effect produced by these four candelabras filled with wax candles, and the becoming light thrown upon every one was very fine. The portly butler in white vest and cravat and black coat, and the groom of the chambers, and a half-dozen or more footmen in red plush and blue coats gave great elegance to the whole effect. I cannot tell you how many kinds of soup there were. Suffice it, that mine was most delicious. Then followed several varieties of fish. The turbot was placed before Mr. Clive. After that came little entrées, delicious patés, and mutton chops, well served. On the side table were every variety of meat — turkeys, chickens, anything you could wish. These courses over, the game followed. I should have told you that the vegetables were cucumbers and asparagus. The service was entirely of silver. The dessert service was of pretty china, but nothing remarkable. The ices and jellies and other most beautifully arranged and delicious dishes were placed on the table. The dessert was composed of every variety of fruit, oranges, pears, grapes, etc.

How often have I dreaded a dinner party! How stiff and formal I have found them to be where people were of no higher rank than my own! And here I was surrounded by the nobles of the land, not having an embarrassed feeling. There was no stiffness, no formality. Nothing could exceed the politeness of Miss Clive, and young Herbert was very agreeable. Full of intelligence he knew and spoke well on every subject. But I was particularly surprised at his knowledge of America. Both Miss Clive and he were so interested and asked me so many questions, and they showed their tact and good-breeding in so many ways. In fact, we were treated with the greatest distinction and the greatest attention, being the honored guests in that distinguished family circle.

Sitting a little while after dessert, Lady Harriet gave the signal to rise and we left the room, Lady Powis preceding on her side of the table and Aunt Catherine on the other. Lady Harriet followed last of all. Passing through the hall, immense colored engravings of the Exhibition were pointed out to us, and then we entered the large and elegant drawing-room. Coffee was brought in, and some of the ladies sat down to their beautiful worsted work, while others disposed themselves around the room. On the walls were many pictures — two Claudes, a Velasquez, and other originals by great artists. In the library was a very fine Murillo. I told Miss Clive how much I had heard of her drawings and how anxious I was to see them, and she in a very kind manner brought in her portfolio of such views in Italy painted in water-colors as I had never seen. She knelt on the floor with a candle in her hand, and showed each one to us. Such skies, such effects, I never imagined to see in water-colors.

Then she brought down a book of views in England, and the only painting in the house by her brother, also in water-colors. Mr. Robert Clive was at Nineveh with Layard, and he showed us a book of lithographs taken from his paintings of the curious sculptures found there. Nothing could exceed their politeness in showing everything that could interest us.

When the gentlemen came in, Lady Harriet Herbert played a beautiful piece by Blumenthal, the author of "Les Deux Anges." Maria and Richard sang some German songs. After these, what do you think was asked for in this aristocratic circle — Negro Melodies!!!! — "The Blue-Tail Fly" and others being received with acclamations of delight. Richard sang the solo parts admirably, and Maria joined in the chorus. Richard was decidedly the most distinguished-looking man in the room, for the Clives and Herberts were all small. The Earl is a little man with rather a bald head.

At eleven we left, having passed the most charming evening you can imagine. Miss Clive is the best, the kindest person in the world. She is not handsome, but she has a fine intelligent face and charming smile. Her sister is very small and plain, but Richard says very agreeable. I must say that never, in all my life, have I been treated with such distinction and kindness by strangers. How different from the New York nonchalance!

I forgot to mention the ceremony of passing the

loving-cup round to the gentlemen at the end of the dinner. A large cup with handles on each side filled with toasted ale is brought in, and the gentleman to whom it is given first takes a long draught, after which the footman passes it to the next gentleman, and so ȯn.

January 3rd, Saturday

THE great event is over, the ball, and I enjoyed myself very much. We did not get to bed until four o'clock this morning. We reached the ball-room at about half-past ten, and found many persons already there. The Clives met us in the kindest and most cordial manner, and Lord Powis immediately engaged me for the first quadrille, and Mr. Robert Clive for the second. The kindness and attention of the family continued throughout the whole evening, and we were taken into their circle — Aunt Catherine occupying a seat at the end of the room near either the Countess or Lady Harriet. I danced every dance, even to the lancers, something new to me and to you. They are nothing more than a new and rather fantastic form of the quadrille. The valse à deux temps, the galop, and polka came in between the quadrille and lancers, but not so often as with us. We have heard so much about the bad manner in which English women dress, but I did not find it so. On the contrary, there were a greater number of well-dressed women than one usually sees at a country ball. The Clives and the Ladies Herbert were exquisitely dressed. Aunt Catherine, too, was charming in a Parisian costume. Lady Powis and Lady Harriet Clive wore superb diamonds. In America I think you see a greater number of pretty faces, and in England of fine shoulders.

The room is large and high, and has a capital floor, and the band was quite good. It is curious to see a public ball so select. You pay at the door seven shillings for the gentleman and five shillings for the ladies, and yet none but gentlemen and ladies were there. I saw the Boughtons, the Keville-Davises of Croft Castle, the Roches of Clungunford, the Cuylers, the Landons, and others — none but the people you would meet at a private house. At the end of the room was a table upon which were tea and cakes, and in an adjoining room oysters and porter for the gentlemen. Lord Powis took Maria to the table and afterwards danced with her. Miss Beale was there and looked remarkably well. It is wonderful how much she makes of herself. She is really a graceful and stylish-looking woman, notwithstanding that Richard when he danced with her looked at least two inches shorter.

I find the Clives so interested about America. Miss Mary Clive told me that she had been studying the map of the United States so that when she asked me what part of it I came from she might know. They read all the American authors — Prescott, Cooper, Irving, and Longfellow are as

familiar to them as to us. There is one thing that
is very odd, however, and that is that they imagine
that everything is on such a grand scale in America
— not only every lake an Ontario, every river a
Mississippi, and every rapid a Niagara, but they
suppose ·our domestic economy grand in propor-
tion. Lady Harriet apologized to Aunt Catherine
for the smallness of her house, and Mrs. Myrick
told Maria that the ballroom must seem very small
to her after the grand ones she had been accustomed to. Maria says she supposes that she has
got some idea into her head about the halls of the
Montezumas. Mr. Robert Clive said to me that
the scenery must seem so confined here in comparison with American views. "Oh, no!" I said to him,
"I suppose our horizon is not more extended than
yours." They appear to think that if they stood
upon a little eminence in any part of the United
States they could see the whole breadth and length
of the Mississippi, Niagara would come dashing
and foaming to their feet, the Rocky Mountains
would tower up as a background, prairies would lie
before them, and the Lakes would come into this
grand *coup d'œil*. To them our horizon is boundless.

At the ball were clergymen, one of whom, Mr.
Longworth, the Vicar of Bromfield, and a bachelor,
asked me to dance, but I was engaged fortunately,
because I should have had some hesitation in dancing with him. Mr. Landon made a very witty,
though it seems to me an irreverent, speech. He

was opening oysters for Uncle Richard when Mr. Longworth called out — "I wish, Landon, you would open some for me." "Oh, no," replied our rector, "I only feed my flock."

Among the beautiful things that I saw at Oakly Park was a gold cup richly ornamented and under a glass case, a present from the Queen to her namesake and godchild, Miss Victoria Clive, a little girl. When the Queen was a little girl she paid a visit to Ludlow and stayed with the Clives.

The Castle of Ludlow belongs to the Earl of Powis, and formerly they had a town house adjoining it, which they now rent. The great Lord Clive accumulated great wealth in India, and at the age of fifty killed himself. His son was created Earl of Powis, an old but extinct title. He married a daughter of the Duke of Montrose, the present Countess Dowager. Some six years ago he was killed by one of his own sons while out shooting. The young man was for a time almost deranged. Lady Lucy is such a sweet pensive-looking creature, and Lady Powis is the most thoroughly elegant and aristocratic-looking woman. She wears her gray hair as Aunt Margaret does, and reminds me very much of her — very much the same figure, though a little stouter, and has not Aunt Margaret's animation.

During the intermission between the dances at the ball I always sat near some one or other of them. On one of these occasions I had a very pleasant conversation with Lady Harriet. She has invited us to come over some fine day to walk about their village and see their school; and Mr. Clive told Maria that we must come over some morning and see Miss Clive paint.

Another honor has been conferred upon us. Yesterday an invitation was received for Mr. and Mrs. and Miss Fay, for the Shrewsbury Hunt Ball, a most select affair, composed entirely of the nobility of Shropshire. Those of the gentry who wish to go must have their names presented ever so long beforehand, and then it requires influence to get them in. Of course we shan't go. Thirty miles is rather too far for a ball where you are a perfect stranger. It was only day before yesterday that Mr. Betton told Uncle Richard that if he wanted an invitation ever so much he could not get it.

Monday, January 5th

I HAVE just come from the most delightful ride with Richard. Uncle Richard bought a new mare on Saturday, and so to-day he proposed I should ride her with Richard, to Bircher Knoll, Miss Beale's. They did not know whether she had ever had a lady on her back before, but I was not to be daunted by that, and I mounted her without fear and found her all I could wish. We went to Miss Beale's, five miles from this, in half an hour, rising to the trot all the way. We found her expecting us, and the bashful Theodore, her brother, came smilingly forward. "Ha, ha! Very happy — ha, ha! to see you." Poor Theodore's blushes are not very becoming to his red hair. He is the most timid man I ever knew. Every time at lunch he asked me to take anything more, it was quite in the Slender style. It was always as if he had premised his — "Will you take some more?" with "I would rather be unmannerly than troublesome," and as if he would receive my refusal with "You do yourself wrong, indeed, la!" His concern because I would not take wine in addition to ale was quite touching. "Indeed, now," he said when my last drop of ale was drunk and I was eating a piece of cake, "you will now, ha, ha! surely, now, you will ha, ha! take a little wine now, ha, ha!" — and he seized the decanter nervously.

I ought to have answered a question of yours some time ago about how Maria likes England. She likes England excessively, in spite of a terrible eruption that she has had since she has been here. There is something peculiar in this climate. I was weighed yesterday, and the man said I weighed eight stones eleven, or one hundred and twenty-three. I think there must be some mistake about it, because I do not look as if I had gained so much.

Thursday, January 8th

WE went to the Myricks' last evening to dinner, and I had quite a nice time. A very plain dinner without pretension. The funniest thing was that

Aunt Catherine was taken in to dinner by the Count of Croymier, the son of a French Marquis and grandson of Lady Sayre, who lives in this neighborhood. He is a dwarf and is hardly so large as a boy of seven years old. He is the smallest man I ever saw, but on account of his rank he was obliged to make himself ridiculous and offer his arm to Aunt Catherine. I did not dare to look at them, but Richard and I looked at each other stealthily. They talk of another public ball in February. In that case I shall have to get a new dress by hook or by crook.

VII

My dear H——:

Four sheets last week have had so little effect in drawing upon my resources that I am all ready to begin again, though this time I certainly cannot hope to have so much to interest you. The ball and the dinner were more fertile subjects than one can always expect to find. We went yesterday to call at Downton Hall, Sir William Boughton's. Unfortunately they were not at home. Nevertheless, I found sufficient compensation in the beauty of the scenery. Two or three miles from Ludlow you find yourself at an exquisitely picturesque gate and lodge. A blooming girl opens the gate and you begin the approach to the house. Winding round, you gradually ascend a range of hills through an avenue two miles long. Sometimes you look down a perpendicular descent into a deep ravine, and through the beautiful trees now stripped of their foliage you have snatches of lovely views. Hilly "crofts" wooded with young trees overhang the road, so that in summer even the sky must be concealed. For two or three miles you traverse this embowered avenue, and when at last the luxurious veil of the boughs and leaves is lifted, you discover what might appear at first sight to be the moss-grown abode of some sylvan goddess. The regularly disposed windows with their white shades, some partly raised and revealing the colored curtains beneath, alone convince you that you are not on enchanted ground. The house, covered with ivy, stands in a semicircle of noble trees and faces a beautiful lawn which runs down to the dingles in the valley. How can I depict to you the glorious scene which breaks upon you as you approach the house! How can I convey to you the beautiful vision that will always remain in my mind's eye, of the cultivated and peaceful valley beneath, of the dells and "bosky dingles" interspersed between the fields of Tilteston, the noble termination of the Clee Hills, which in themselves would make a lovely landscape! But when, in addition, you have a view of our own Mary Knoll and the Vignyles in the distance, you can imagine that there is nothing wanting to add to the beauty of the scene.

January 15th

I AM writing to you at eleven o'clock A.M., having arrived home this morning at half-past four o'clock, after a dinner and dance at Henley Hall, Sir Charles Cuyler's. At seven o'clock last evening we were put down before the door of this fine old place. It is by no means kept in the style of Oakly Park or Downton Hall, for Sir Charles has a moderate fortune and an immense family. Still, we were received in the hall by liveried footmen, and while we were taking off our cloaks we had time to observe the magnificent stags' heads, brought from the Cape, and even shot by Sir Charles himself, which hung upon the walls. The butler led us through a long narrow passageway and throwing open the door announced us. We found the party already assembled, and consisting of Sir Charles and Lady Cuyler; two Miss Cuylers; Mr. Frederick Cuyler; Sir William Boughton; Miss Boughton and her *dame de compagnie*, Madame Eichbaum; Count de Croymier; Mr. Clarke, the lawyer; and a Mr. Church. The effect, perhaps, as we entered, was less imposing than at Oakly Park, but more home-like and most antique. The large room, panelled with oak to the ceiling; the low but richly orna-mented ceiling itself, the finely carved mantel-piece, the antique chairs, the portraits on the walls, among which was one of a lady by Sir Godfrey Kneller, and another of Sir Charles's father. Then distributed about the room were antique ornaments of all kinds, china, carvings, and other curiosities which I could have continued to observe and ad-mire if dinner had not been announced.

It is curious how strictly the etiquette of pre-cedence is observed here — even so far that Miss Boughton was taken in to dinner by Sir Charles and seated on his left, and again poor Aunt Cath-erine was sacrificed to the rank of the little Count, and followed Sir Charles, and was seated on his right. Uncle Richard led in Madame Eich-

baum, who, though *dame de compagnie* to Miss
Boughton and possessing an unpronounceable German name, is both a lady and an Englishwoman,
as fine-looking as she is cultivated, ladylike,
and kind. Uncle Richard sat at the other end of
the table at the right of Lady Cuyler, and next to
Madame Eichbaum sat Mr. Clarke, who was un-
provided with a lady. Maria and Mr. Church filled
up the vacancy on that side of the table. On our
side, Richard sat next to Miss Boughton, and
beside him Constance Cuyler whom he had taken
in to dinner. Frederick Cuyler and I came next,
and Miss Cuyler and Mr. Longworth. Beside
Lady Cuyler at the foot of the table was Sir William Boughton, a large, stout, red-faced, white-
haired, gouty old gentleman. Lady Cuyler, though
the mother of thirteen children, is still a fresh and
beautiful woman. Miss Boughton I do not very
much admire. Her face is plain and high-colored;
her figure is fine and stylish. She dresses well and
has a good manner, and dances admirably. Constance Cuyler is sweetly pretty, but her sisters are
uncommonly plain. Thus you have the party before you.

The dining-room is rather large, and the walls
panelled with oak. The table was in good style —
silver centre-piece and plated candelabras. The
dishes were of silver and placed upon the table, but
the plates were of painted china. A rich white soup
first came on; then cod's head and shoulders; after-

wards boiled turkey and venison for the large dishes, preceded, however, by various entrées and accompanied by vegetables. Game followed in due course — hare and pheasants. Here the dessert is placed on the table with the game, and if you do not take game, creams, jellies, etc., are handed to you immediately and in succession. Before the first cloth is removed, grated cheese and cheese cut into pieces, biscuits and bread, and little pats of butter are served. After this come the fruits, fresh and dried, and nuts, etc., more properly, I suppose, called the dessert. It is customary, when you go to dine, to take your own butler or footman, and he offers his services to wait. They are accepted except at a place like Oakly Park or, I suppose, Downton Hall — so there were quite a number of menservants, among whom I recognized the Boughton livery. About nine o'clock we retired to the drawing-room, leaving the dining-room to the gentlemen.

I am getting very fond of dinner parties. When I have discussed hunting in all its phases with Frederick Cuyler, I turn to Mr. Longworth (the Vicar of Bromfield), who, though a coarse man, is very pleasant and always quite attentive to me. There is nothing like strictness or formality at these English dinners. Every one talks to his neighbor in a low tone, or even across the table. You are not introduced, but that makes no difference. It was some time before I found out who were taking me in to dinner. Coffee is brought into the drawing-room to the ladies, and when the gentlemen come in tea and little cakes are handed round.

The Landons arrived at half-past nine o'clock, and at ten the Myricks came, which completed the party. We had first some singing on the part of Mr. Church and Miss Cuyler. They sang "Would that my Love," without expression, or rather in the most die-away manner, and then half a tone or more too flat. After that they tried a difficult duet in "La Favorita," in which they were equally unsuccessful. Richard and Maria are great favorites. Their German songs are listened to with the greatest attention and pleasure, and then their negro melodies are always called for. Indeed, Richard has, I think, quite won the hearts of all the young ladies here by his elegant manners and appearance and his delightful dancing. Sir Charles was in great spirits, and not only proposed dancing immediately, but opened the ball himself. Valses, as they say here, polkas, and the lancers, followed in succession. I was engaged so deep that it was a long time before I could give Richard a dance. I danced twice with the little Count. Fancy how short he must be that my chin rested occasionally on his hair. After supper we had a valse, polka, and quadrille, and then the cotillion. The little Count led that quite admirably. Indeed, his air was martial and magnificent as he directed, and though "he be little he is fierce." He has a formidable moustache and looks his age of twenty-seven. We had a delightful evening, and I was unwilling to leave at four o'clock. We got to bed at five, so you can fancy I had not much sleep, as I got up at half-past eight. Nevertheless, I took a walk next day and felt as fresh as possible. You would have enjoyed it so much. How I wish you were here! Sir Charles is so gay and so determined that every one shall be happy. It is delightful to see the old gentleman dancing in the old-fashioned style, and to watch his little portly person tripping about on the light fantastic toe. I had but one regret, and that was that I was engaged when he asked me to dance. Uncle Richard displayed great patience in staying through the cotillion, though he would willingly have been at home and abed. Aunt Catherine enjoys dancing as much as we do.

January 17th

SIR WILLIAM BOUGHTON invited us at Henley to come over to lunch with him at Downton Hall, and then he would go with us to Downton Castle. Yesterday being the appointed day, you can imagine with what delight we hailed the sun as it shone into the window. Its promises were not deceitful, for nothing could have been finer or better suited to such a purpose than the whole day. Just as we got through breakfast Mr. Joseph Gardner arrived. He is a young man, the son of Mr. and Mrs. John

L. Gardner of Boston, intimate friends of Aunt
Catherine, and has come from America bent on the
grand tour. He had hardly time to breakfast and
dress before it was time to start. Richard went on
horseback, and Uncle Richard remained at home
to ferret rabbits. The drive seemed very short, for
Mr. Gardner gave us an entertaining account of his
voyage and much Boston chit-chat. We found ourselves in due time at the hall, and were received in
a fine large room by Madame Eichbaum and the
two Miss Boughtons. Sir William, in blue coat,
gilt buttons, and buff waistcoat, soon came hob-
bling in and soon set to work, it seemed to me, to
pump Mr. Gardner. I am sorry to say that the
Right Honorable Sir William Rouse-Boughton,
Baronet, is evidently a domestic tyrant. His
daughters seem to stand in awe of him and his
caprices are humored in every way. We had often
a confidential whisper from Madame Eichbaum —
"You must admire this. It is a pet of Sir William's."
Or, "Sir William did this — he will be particularly
pleased with your admiration."

I drove in the Boughtons' carriage from the
hall to the castle, some seven miles, and as it was
an open carriage Sir William sat on the box beside
the coachman and drove, so that it was particularly
necessary to give me these hints. I did, however,
notwithstanding all this caution, contrive to admire the wrong tower as we approached the castle.
In my enthusiasm I exclaimed as I caught sight of

an embattled moss-grown tower — "How lovely, how——" when Madame Eichbaum whispered, "You must admire the other, Sir William built it," and the unfinished exclamation was addressed to the new tower.

But I have sadly digressed from the lunch. It was served in a very fine room, they say altogether more beautifully embellished than any dining-room in the neighborhood. That at Oakly Park is grander, as far as size is concerned, but not so rich. The walls are painted a greenish-gray, and upon them are beautiful ornaments in plaster, *in relievo*. Sir William says that the carving, which is fine, was all done by hand. Some admirable portraits are inserted into the walls, and around them, instead of gilt frames, are frames *in relievo* and white plaster corresponding to the other ornamental work. The whole produces a very beautiful, and to me novel, effect. After lunch we walked about the grounds until the ladies got ready. We saw a golden Scotch eagle in an iron cage in the open air, and Richard brought away one of his feathers as a trophy.

At last we were safely placed in the carriages, and Sir William took us first to see his limestone quarry. We were surprised to find that under the avenue were several long subterranean galleries, one on top of another. Everything had been arranged for our visit, for Sir William is particularly proud of this work, as it has all been his own. Not only has he excavated these long galleries, but he has built a little railway which runs the entire length of the lower and newer gallery. Aunt Catherine, Maria, and myself were placed in a little car, and then the head man, pushing from behind, ran us down into what seemed, to my limited experience, the bowels of the earth. Were it not for candles placed here and there and appearing like so many bright points in the distance, it would have been as dark as Erebus. Sir William and the rest of the party followed on foot. We were requested to admire the stone work at the entrance, and the peculiarity of the stratification, being perpendicular; and, indeed, the whole work we were expected to consider very wonderful. And so it was, I know, only it is well to have a cue occasionally.

At last, having used as many terms of admiration and wonder as we could think of, the which if I should write would fill this page with points of exclamation, we got into the carriages and were soon on the way to the castle. Here again I was called upon to admire what Sir William pleased. "Observe," said he, as we drew up to the lodge belonging to the hall, "that though the chimney appears to come out of the centre of the house, it is not built at the centre, but at the side, and by means of arches it appears where it is." And as I was the only one of our family in the carriage, I had to admire for them and myself, too. Occasionally Sir William would stop the carriage to let the others most lovely country, we entered the lodge gates of the castle, which are far inferior to the rest of the place and too near the house. For the first time, however, I saw a veritable castle, although it is of quite recent date. It was built by a Mr. Knight, who, finding that an immense house did not give happiness or comfort, built for himself three little apartments at the back of the castle, beyond the offices and servants' hall, and to which he had a private entrance. Finally, he left the castle and inhabited a little cottage, and gave the splendid demesne to his brother, the father of Lady Boughton. The castle, with ten thousand pounds a year, goes to Sir William's second son.

I do not know how to describe it to you, to give an adequate idea of its size. Sir William had it warmed for us. There is one great defect in the entrance. Instead of entering a fine hall, you find yourself in a vestibule, and thence you proceed to a long and narrow corridor at the end of which is a sitting-room hung with pictures. From this room you enter on one side a suite of apartments composed of two immense drawing-rooms and a dining-room. The fine effect of these was injured by the want of much of the furniture and the absence of carpets, for Sir William is repairing and improving. The walls are hung with magnificent pictures, but so little did Miss Boughton know about them that she told me that in the centre drawing-room there was a Titian, but she could not point it out. However, we saw a Correggio, a Teniers, some of Morland's, and many other rare works of art.

In the front drawing-room were four pillars of porphyry, and rich Italian marbles exquisitely carved adorned the mantelpieces. The dining-room is very grand, being the height of both stories, with a dome of glass by which the room is lighted. On the other side of the sitting-room was, I think, a bedchamber, an exquisite little boudoir. Upstairs were bedrooms of any number and variety. There was the state bedroom where Queen Victoria, when a Princess, washed her hands. The peculiarity of a state bedroom is not that it is so much better than the other bedrooms, but that the bed is placed in a recess.

Sir William mounted with us to the top of the house where the view does not please me as much as many that I have seen about here — too confined, too shut in by hills. After we descended, we went through all the offices, the dairy, the pantries, the pastry-room, the kitchen, the servants' hall, the larder, etc., etc., and Richard and I went into the stables. We did not walk about the grounds, for we had too little time to see both the house and the grounds; the latter can be seen at any time without Sir William as cicerone. After having passed a most delightful day, we reached home at six o'clock, just in time for dinner. We had but one thing to regret, and that was the loss of a visit from Lady Harriet.

21st of January

BEFORE I write another word I must acknowledge the receipt of two letters from you. I was made very anxious by knowing that Clara had had scarlet fever, for there has been a very sad death here of it. All the Bridges have been ill with it, and one of the sons who came home for the Christmas holidays died after two days' illness last week. I was glad to know that Clara was well again.

Uncle Richard sometimes talks of going to America next month. It is impossible to say when he will go, or if he will go at all. I find that I can have a dress quite tolerably done at Ludlow. If I go out any more, I shall get a tulle, which is only one shilling a yard. It is necessary at the smallest dinner to be in full ball dress. I find that I was correctly weighed. Twenty pounds in three months is a pretty good gain. I made some inquiries the other day about cloths for habits, and I found I could get the most beautiful broadcloth, such as the ladies use here for habits, for about twelve shillings a yard, or sixteen dollars for the whole habit.

It is too bad that you should complain of my letter. If it were not interesting, it was because I tried very hard in the absence of incident to make it so. You know I never assumed any airs as a letter-writer. If my first letters were interesting, it was more from the circumstances under which they were written than from any merit of mine. No one could have been more astonished than I was at the compliments I received from you.

Last Saturday we went to lunch with Mr. Charlton to see that sweetest and quaintest of all places, Ludford. On the outside it looks like a jail, with its grated windows, so that once a Scotchman, seeing the dairymaid at the window as he passed, said, "Ah, lassie, ye are there for nae gude." It is built around an open square, and you drive through a heavy gateway into the courtyard. You think you are about entering a gloomy place, but, once in the drawing-room and looking upon the lovely and smiling lawn without the square, so to speak, you can imagine nothing so genial, so cheerful, so sunny. Almost in the midst of a town, you have on this side of the house the profound repose, the park-like aspect of a remote country place. Ludford was an ancient monastery, and adjoining it is the beautiful parish church. The banqueting-hall is exactly as it was left by the monks, even to the black-letter books out of which they read while they were at their meals. There is the same narrow open table in the centre, the same stall-like seats against the walls. Sir Job Charlton entertained King James the First and his Queen at Ludford, and I sat down in the same chair which they had used. We saw the bedchamber the King occupied, and any number of quaint rooms.

In every direction we met the visages of the deceased Charltons and Lechmeres. It was funny to hear Mr. Charlton talk about his ancestors. He says he is the representative of two of the oldest families in the kingdom, the Lechmeres and the Charltons, and yet any day he would sell his whole pedigree for a sandwich, if he were hungry. He could satisfy our curiosity about very few of the portraits. Sir Francis Charlton's portrait he pointed out as having some merit, having been painted by Sir Joshua Reynolds. Another of Sir Job, who entertained King James, and still another he noticed because he had been the great man of the family, Sir Blundell by name. Sir Job lies in red robes on his monument in the church, and around are the mortal remains of his ancestors and descendants.

We went to church on Sunday at Ludford. Whatever may be the example of the clergy, the laity are as devout as the former are neglectful and irreverent. Mr. Charlton, the racing, fox-hunting squire, is the most reverential devout Christian you can imagine. There was one peculiarity about the clergymen that was very funny. It is the custom here for the clergymen to wear black gloves always in the reading-desk and sometimes in the pulpit. This parson, however, instead of wearing kid gloves, encased his hands in plush ones, which as they hung over the pulpit looked like bear's paws, much to the disgust of Mr. Charlton.

Mr. Charlton comes often to play whist, and Maria and Aunt Catherine grow every time more tenderly attached to him. As on these occasions I play chess with Richard, I lose many of his most charming anecdotes and sententious remarks. I am quite set up in my own opinion, since he complimented my riding and said I had a capital seat, for it is not often he says any one rides well.

We find Mr. Gardner very pleasant, but he has not Frank Peabody's sweet ways. Apropos of Frank, what was my surprise to meet him in the park Sunday week, accompanied by his friend Mr. Richard Hunt, who is likewise at the École des Beaux Arts in Paris.

In consequence of the rain in the morning, I stayed at home with Willie, for the carriage could not hold us all. As they were returning, the carriage was stopped and Frank's smiling face put in at the window. He had arrived in the morning and was staying at the Feathers Inn in Ludlow. It seems that he enjoyed himself so much here at Christmas that after his return to Paris he induced his friend Mr. Hunt to come to England and to Ludlow. They remained until Tuesday noon, but I do not think Frank enjoyed himself as at first, though the Landons spent Monday evening here and we had dancing. However, the Landons found Mr. Hunt quite as entertaining as Frank.

VIII

My dear H——:

Though I shall be careful to suppress the prose
Pegasus, I doubt whether I shall be able to make
this letter worth your reading. Unlucky Pegasus!
When I mounted him it was with trepidation lest
I had not the skill to manage him. I dare say his
wings were clipped, and therefore he refused when
I attempted to put him over some ignoble hurdle
which stood in the way of a magnificent flight. I
shall consign him to abler hands, and in the meantime I will remember what Pope says —

"Launch not beyond your depth, but be discreet,
  And mark that point where sense and dullness meet."

Let me premise, however, the record of the days
that have elapsed since I last wrote, by warning you
that you cannot always have incidents. The time
must be occasionally when I cannot satisfy your
rapacious appetite with food more dainty than
some stray thoughts grown in a very barren soil.

On Friday, we went to return a visit at Croft
Castle, the residence of Mr. and Mrs. Keville-
Davis. It is one of the finest places about here,
whatever Sir William Boughton may say of Downton Castle. For the extent of park, the beauty of
the trees which form the avenue, and the scenery

around it, it is infinitely finer than anything I have seen. The castle itself is very beautiful, portions of it being very old, and even the more modern parts are ancient enough to be very picturesque. The terrace, the gardens, and the shrubbery are exquisite. Mrs. Davis was unfortunately not at home.

Joe Gardner left early Saturday morning in a post-chaise. He is going to travel all over Europe and is even determined to penetrate Russia and go up the Nile. Unfortunately, Uncle Richard had appointed Saturday for a shooting party. I say unfortunately, because a few moments after Sir Charles arrived it began to pour. Keepers, beaters, and dogs were kept in a state of preparation until after lunch when the gentlemen sallied out for a short time and came in drenched. Until lunch, with the exception of while they were playing a game of billiards, we had the gentlemen in the drawing-room, that is, Sir Charles and Captain Russell. Somebody told Sir Charles that in his shooting dress he looked like Cock Robin with his tail pulled out, and you cannot imagine a better picture of him. Captain Russell is a handsome man, black eyes and black hair, and black moustache, and a fine color, and he evidently thinks that if he found it worth his while he might be irresistible. As it is, he does not speak unless he is addressed, and then in a soft low voice he replies and rolls his eyes up at you, so there is nothing left for you to do but to cast yours down as if blinded. I had the pleasure of sitting next to him at the table and afterwards entertaining him while the others played whist, until I was called to take Maria's place while she went to the piano. Fancy with what pleasure I play, for Sir Charles and Uncle Richard are perfect whist-players and always bet sixpence a point, so that every trick is of great importance. Although I have improved, I play by no means well. However, I usually have good luck.

I do not think I told you that poor Charles Landon was to go to London to be admitted to the University there. He is to be a clergyman, and the idea in sending him to London was that they wanted students so much that he would be likely to have a less severe examination than at Oxford or Cambridge. He has been studying for some time, poor fellow, as hard as he could, and it was necessary that he should know the Thirty-nine Articles and have some general idea of the Bible. I have never, I believe, given you to understand that Charles was a person of very brilliant parts, but still I myself was not prepared for the account of the examination. He returned Saturday, having failed principally in the Scriptures. You can have some idea of how well he was prepared for the ministry, for when asked who were cast into the fiery furnace, he replied, "Abraham, Isaac, and Jacob." Edward confided this and other equally brilliant replies to me on Sunday. Charles pleaded illness and stayed at home and out of sight. I suppose he was mortified, poor fellow.

I went twice to Richard's castle to church on Sunday, and had the pleasure of getting dripping wet on returning from the afternoon service. I suffered no ill effects from it, however. I should not be surprised to tell you the next time I am weighed that I am fast approaching one hundred and thirty. I can actually see the gradual increase. Apropos of this, Charles Landon addressed a new and entirely original remark to me yesterday. His usual salutation is — "Well, Miss Anna Maria, and how are you getting on?" but yesterday it was — "Well, Miss Anna Maria, have you been getting weighed lately?" — which so startled me that I thought it must be significant of something; so I hastened to say "No," and add, "Why do you ask?" But he immediately relapsed into his usually meaningless and indefinite manner, and said, "Oh, nothing."

February 1st

THIS is the last day of shooting. Birds, rabbits, and hares may still continue to be the prey of the sportsman. They, poor things, have no respite. Yesterday Richard and I took a charming ride. We have the sun about once a week, and yesterday was one of those days when after alternate storm and sunshine the day ends magnificently. We started with the intention of going across country, which means going through the fields, sometimes through gates and sometimes over hedges. We found all the gates locked, so that we had to begin with a hedge. Do not think that in taking a hedge I go with a flying leap. Not at all. Richard goes over first and breaks the way for me. The hedge is planted on a bank, with a ditch always on one side. So I put Romeo at it, but he makes a point of refusing the first time. However, a good cut of the whip and a resolute hand brings him at it again. This time he scrambles up the bank, pushes his head through the hedge, gathers his feet together as well as he can, while I collect my habit around me, throw myself back in the saddle, give a determined blow with the whip, let his head go, and away we clear the ditch! It was thus we got into some fields and thus we had to leave them, for we found we were where we ought not to be. However, we were not to be daunted in our determination of going across country, and trying the other side we soon found ourselves in a field where the turf was so delightful that we started at once into a gallop. Richard led the way, and I observed that, as he went over a ditch ahead of us, it was a good stretch even for his horse. Still I was rash enough not to slacken my speed, so that poor little Romeo had to give a jump in the air in order to clear it, which threw me so completely out of my seat that I could not recover my balance, and slipping my foot out of the stirrup in another moment I was on the ground. Imagine Richard's state of mind. He saw the queer jump Romeo gave, observed that I was in my seat as we cleared the ditch, but the next look showed me in the act of going over. However, I had picked myself up before he could get to me, entirely unhurt. I told him that mine was that "vaulting ambition which o'erleaps itself and falls on the other side." If I had taken the ditch at a moderate pace, as I always do, I should not have had the tumble. I was careful to say nothing of my adventure at home, except to Maria, who has not ridden since the day she fell off Juliet without the slightest provocation, and found herself hanging by the stirrup. Her appearance on horseback was always the signal for a roar of laughter on the part of the Landons.

The pleasure of our ride was not in the least affected by my fall. The day was glorious, and as we went round by the Goggin, climbing up by steep footpaths, then across country, up on Hanway, we looked down, now on a deep ravine with the variegated cultivated hillsides all around, running down to it; now on a broad rich valley with the Clee Hills and the Welsh Hills in the distance. It is thus that Richard and I ride almost every day. We take some bypath or lane that leads we know not where, and we follow it over hill, over dale, with the Vignyles always for our beacon. You can conceive of nothing like the profound solitude that reigns around us in these rides. Here and there we see a cottage with the smoke curling up, but that is the only sign of life except that every now and then a dog expresses his displeasure at our intrusion by a feeble bark. In every direction we see the fruits of labor and of wonderful care, but we see nothing of the laborer or cultivator. Often we pass through hamlets without meeting a soul.

Richard thinks it a great bore to ride with women, as a general thing, for they are either so timid that you must almost hold their reins, or else they must go on a hard gallop all the time. Of course I am an exception. I believe Richard only makes the remark to prove the exception. I am sure that timidity is the last thing that I can be accused of. I am content to go quietly over steep or bad paths, I like to trot upon the road, and to gallop upon the turf. You cannot know the pleasures of riding until you go over the turf. Your horse becomes as much inspirited as yourself. The soft turf is like velvet to his feet, and he carries you along as it were upon the wings of the wind. It leaves me but one thing to wish, and that is that I might be following a pack of hounds. The other day Richard and I galloped across the fields with Mr. Charlton and two couples of greyhounds to find a hare to course, and though without success, I imagine what my excitement would be were I following fifteen or twenty couples of fox-hounds or harriers. You would be surprised at the extent of my sporting knowledge. Indeed, it is quite necessary here. A young man takes you in to dinner whom you do not know. You exhaust the weather, but there is always a resource for you, for it is always apropos to say — "Capital day for scent," or the reverse. You are then treated to a description of the run which interests me as much as it does the young man himself. If fox-hounds, he tells me of how many coverts were drawn blank; where the fox was found; where viewed, if he ran to earth, and how he got out; if they drew blood; and who was in at the death. Mr. Erasmus Salway is the Master of a pack of harriers and hunts this manor very often. It is not so exciting or so dangerous as fox-hunting. The hare neither runs to cover nor to earth, as they say; that is, does not go into the woods nor into holes, but runs in circles of three or four miles. There is nothing finer than a pack of hounds in full cry.

I can imagine that you would find the life here dull because you can neither walk much nor ride, for those, after all, are our chief amusements.

I draw or write every morning until lunch. Then after lunch I always go out unless it rains hard, often read to Aunt Catherine in the evening, and sew or play games until the children go to bed, then Richard and I play chess. We go to Ludlow about once a week, and now that the Landons don't come every day, our visitors are few and far between.

Uncle Richard talks of going home the middle of this month, but it is impossible to count upon his movements. He dreads the cold of New England. I am writing to you with the windows open, though it is raining hard. What a contrast to your climate ten degrees south of us!

February 4th

WE had a long-standing invitation from Lady Harriet to go to Oakly Park yesterday to lunch, and to walk about the grounds and visit the schools. You can therefore understand with what pleasure we hailed the sun as he rose in a clear sky. No Savannah day could have been more lovely. The touch of frost in the air prevented it from being springlike, and made out-of-door exercise delicious. The Clee Hills put on their best look, and Mary Knoll and the Vignyles, always more sombre, assumed a more smiling aspect than usual. The earth seemed to have excelled herself in a fresher green. And thus, with so much to enjoy on our way, and so much pleasure in anticipation in meeting the Clives once more, we found ourselves again received in the vestibule by the portly butler, and the footmen, this time in undress livery, blue coats and silver buttons, gray tights and unpowdered heads.

The door of the same fine library was open, but no elegant circle rose to receive us, and we spent a few moments preceding Lady Harriet's appearance in examining a beautiful Murillo over the mantelpiece, a boy playing with a lamb. When Lady Harriet did appear, it was with the same elegant and dignified manner and with the same kindness which had charmed us before. Soon Miss Clive came in, then Miss Mary Clive and an elderly lady whom we found afterwards to be Mrs. Stackhouse-Acton, of Acton Scott, sister of the late Lady Boughton.

After our mutual congratulations upon the auspicious weather, regrets at not having met before since the ball, descriptions of what had been going on in the meantime, and much pleasant small talk, we were taken into the drawing-room to see the Claudes and other fine pictures. One of the Claudes is of rare beauty and remarkable for its silver light. The beautiful pictures, the articles of vertu, and fine cabinets are the adornments of this room.. The tables, chairs, sofas, and divans are all plain, but rich and substantial — nothing for show, but everything for use and comfort. We found so much to admire that time passed quickly, and, it seemed to me, lunch was announced very soon after we had arrived.

Lunch was served without ceremony. We did not even wait for the gentlemen to make their appearance. It was quite the ladies' affair. The table contained everything that was nice, cutlets, pheasant, chicken, cold round of beef, and other cold meats, which I could not see, besides vegetables — asparagus, sea-kale, beans, Brussels sprouts, etc. Pudding and tarts, fruits and cake completed the repast. After we were seated, Mr. Clive and Mr. Robert Clive came in, the former going round and shaking hands in his soft way. Lady Harriet said grace and returned thanks as we rose from the table. We spent a few moments in examining the dining-room, and particularly a beautiful statue of Hagar in the Wilderness and a picture of the great Lord Clive.

Before going out to walk Miss Clive took Maria and myself upstairs, Aunt Catherine and Lady Harriet having preceded us. We were shown Lady Harriet's sitting-room, full of comforts and pictures and books, but plain and simple. Then we went into the state bedroom, the furniture of which was made at Bromfield. Indeed, Miss Clive says they have everything done there that can be. Afterwards we ascended another story to Miss Clive's bedroom. There the same simplicity characterizes the furniture, but what particularly amused us was a spinning-wheel in the corner. Every evening from six to seven the young ladies spin with the German governess in the drawing-room. They have a weaver in the village who converts all their yarn into huckaback for towels. They are never idle, and do a great deal of worsted work, and we saw in a frame in Miss Clive's room a cashmere scarf which she was embroidering in the Turkish style.

When we returned to the drawing-room, we found that the rest of the party had gone to the conservatory, where we followed them through several little rooms which I do not remember well enough to describe. At last a glass door admits us into a conservatory, but already a delicious fragrance pervades the air and gives us a foretaste of what we are to enjoy. Here lovely and rare plants admirably placed, and many in bloom, made this as delightful as conservatories always are. I recognized some old friends, particularly the Popignac (acacia). From the conservatory we went into a garden, thence into a rockery where rough rocks are made to contribute to beauty in grottoes and other picturesque arrangements. Afterwards we went to see the sundial supported by a fine Egyptian figure, and to examine some curious varieties of firs and pines.

Nothing surprised me more than the varied acquirements of these English women. Lady Harriet is as well acquainted with trees and botany as few men are in our country. She knows every tree on the place, and so in fact does Miss Clive. Since I have been here I have learned to appreciate the value and beauty of trees, a thing so utterly disregarded in America. Perhaps some centuries hence the ruthless havoc made in our forests will be regretted. Posterity, perhaps, will sorrow as much over the work of the treadmills at the railway stations as the poor horses do now.

I am not going to give you a dissertation on this subject. On the contrary, I shall stop here and at the same time take leave of Mr. Clive, Uncle Richard, and Mr. Robert Clive, who go to walk over the model farm, while the rest of us pursue our winding way to the school, passing along by the banks of the Teme near which grow the magnificent Druidical oaks of which I have written before. Then over a rustic bridge to the common on which stands the church.

The school is over an old archway, once the entrance to an ancient priory, the remains of which adjoin the church. Hard by is the mill which makes the air vocal with its monotonous buzzing. A narrow flight of stairs admits us into the schoolroom in which the children rise as we enter. The room is long and the chimney stands in the centre, or perhaps I should have said two thirds the length of the room. The roof is timbered and the whole effect is quaint. You might imagine that such might have been the room in which the schoolmaster taught the rustics of "Sweet Auburn, loveliest village of the plain." The ages of the girls appear to range from four or five to twelve or thirteen. They were all dressed in stuff dresses and spotlessly white aprons. Their hair was smooth, and their hands perfectly clean. Indeed, so careful is Lady Harriet that they should be clean that the means are provided for repairing any mischief to hair or hands that the walk to school might have produced. Each child has, too, a pair of list shoes to provide against sitting in damp ones. The boys were much younger than the girls, or rather they were all small, for the elder ones have to go into the fields. The ladies took the greatest pleasure in showing us the copy-books of the older girls and the slates of the little ones who were just learning. We examined the sewing of these, the marking of those, and the sums of the numberless little urchins. Then they sang for us admirably, one or more of the elder girls taking the second part. Nothing can be more judicious than the whole management. A monitor is appointed from among the elder girls, who takes care of the school, washes any towels that may be used, and performs any domestic office that may be required. Each has a string attached to the slate that hangs around the neck. When they get through using them, the monitor goes around and says — "String." Immediately the string is taken off and held in the hands. Again she says — "Slate." Each slate is handed to her and is put away. When the girls are fourteen or fifteen, they go out to service in Ludlow or the neighborhood, and if they do well Lady Harriet recommends them whenever she can. She is equally careful to provide amusements for them. In the yard was a swing and gymnastic exercises. At Christmas they have a Christmas tree upon which each child finds a present, and a tea party accompanies the festival.

It is thus that these noble English women adorn their station. Miss Clive takes the greatest pleasure in visiting the cottages, and she knows every man, woman, and child by name. In the Sunday school are seventy scholars, and the young ladies teach them there. It is delightful to see the good the Clives do, and then they are so charming in themselves, and so happy in each other. They treat one another with such politeness and such affection. Thorough good breeding pervades every act, every detail. I hope I may take to heart and practice all that I have learned from them in these respects. We had the pleasure of again seeing Miss Clive's drawings, and some of Lady Harriet's, who paints even better than Miss Clive. We were to have gone to Ludlow to sketch at the castle yesterday, with Miss Clive and Mrs. Stackhouse-Acton, but the rain prevented. As you can imagine, we passed the most charming day at Oakly Park. Indeed, I look with a double glance at everything — one for the present and another for the future.

I must hurry to a close, as it is nearly time for the bag to go.

IX

My DEAR W——:

Your letter ought to have been answered long ago, but H.'s letters take up so much of my time that I have little time for others.

I often wish you were here — you would enjoy so much going out with Uncle Richard. This morning Lily came into our room before we were quite dressed, to tell us to come and see thirteen pheasants before the dining-room window. They are beautiful birds, almost as large, if not quite, as chickens, and run about the grounds very tamely. The cock pheasant has very brilliant plumage, and, when you pick one up, he makes a tremendous noise.

The season for shooting birds is over, but Uncle Richard enjoys very much ferreting rabbits; you would enjoy this very much. A ferret is a little gray or white animal which they use instead of a dog. They sew up the poor thing's mouth; otherwise it would eat the rabbit, and attend more to its own appetite than to the pleasure of the sportsman. The keeper puts a string around its neck, places it at a hole, and soon you hear a rumbling in the earth and in a trice a rabbit pops out the other entrance to its house. The sportsman stands ready with his gun, and poor Bunny no sooner escapes from one enemy than he falls a victim of another still more relentless. His hapless body is thrown into the bag, is carried tŏ the larder with his unfortunate companions, and hung up by the legs, till the cook thinks that it is time he should be either smothered with onions or be made a pie of, in which latter form I frequently discuss his merits at breakfast or luncheon.

Yesterday we went to see hares coursed, which is a very nice sport. Several couples of greyhounds are leashed together, that is, they are so fastened together that the instant the signal is given by the beaters, with one jerk the straps are drawn out of the buckles, and they start at the same moment, free of each other. Men with long sticks beat the coverts, and the moment the hare breaks, a couple of hounds start in full chase. Away flies Pussy across the field, close pursued, and woe betide if she does not find shelter in the first covert she sees, for greyhounds run by sight and not by smell, so she is safe when the bushes conceal her from view. Though five hares broke cover yesterday, only one was coursed, and that one was not caught. The others got too far away before the hounds were loosed. So, my dear W., notwithstanding the game preserves, which has given you so great a disgust for England, you would find much to amuse you here.

Maria wants to add a few lines to H.

X

My dear J——:[1]

I confess to feeling not a little surprise at not hearing from you, particularly as I attempted to hold out the alluring hope of a schedule of the organ stops, and my invaluable hints and remarks upon church music, not knowing, of course, that you had awakened at last to the charms of our now happy sex. I could not hope for a delicate attention in the shape of a letter on the score of my own merits, and as your cousinly regard for my welfare could always be satisfied by H. and H.'s letters, I feared that I was not to hear from you at all, but I am as generous as I am candid, and I hasten to repair the foul wrong I did you by answering your letter at once and thanking you for the affection expressed in it.

I often think of you and wish it were your ear, instead of mine, which tries to arrive at the exact quality of Sesquialtera Diapason, etc. Maria and I made a flying visit one day to the organ loft, and managed to scribble down on the blank leaf of my Prayer-Book a list of the stops. It is curious that this organ was built by the very man who built the old one at Christ Church of our Cambridge, Snetzler. Here, then, are the stops:

[1] Mr. John Wilcox.

Right hand — Principal Swell, Hauteboy Swell, Trumpet Swell, Dulciana Choir, Flute Choir, Open Diapason Choir, Furniture Gr., Sesquialtera Gr., Cornet Gr., Stopt Diapason Gr., Pedal Pipes.

Left hand — Swell Coupler, Open Diapason, Stopt Diapason, Principal Choir, Stopt Diapason Choir, Trumpet Choir, 15th Gr., 12th Gr., Principal Gr., Open Diapason Gr.

You know better than I the merits of this combination. All I can do is to compare, as well as my limited experience will permit, the qualities of each stop with what you have taught me ought to be its proper characteristic, and such as Mr. Hook's organs possess. The misfortune is that the organ is badly played and its powers not yet brought out, but it strikes me that the swell is not powerful. But the organ is in a large church, and, compared with ours, the bass does not appear sufficiently powerful. I say these things with fear and trembling, in all humility, and I leave you to judge, by your former experience of my opinions on such subjects, of how much value this may be.

There are some good voices in the choir, and they sing well, that is, in time and together — but the pointing of the chants — my dear J., I can imagine that, in the process of gabbling over some words and drawling out others to a most interminable length, you would find yourself in your agony rolled up in a ball. For example, they always read the Venite and chant the Te Deum, because it gives the clergyman a rest between the lessons, and sometimes, when they do not sing Jackson in F, they use the simple double chant, which leaves them at liberty to divide the words for themselves. Thus they sing, "Thou art the King of Glory, Oh .... Oh .... Oh .... Christ." Shocking, is it not? And so on through the whole chant. Let me advise you to suggest to Mr. L. to sing the Te Deum and read the Venite. Mr. Merrick says it is such a rest. They always sing the Gloria Patri after every psalm in the Psalter, and when there is no singing it is read. Instead of a sentence, as we have before the service, they have an anthem or hymn.

At Ludlow they are exceedingly fond of "Peace, troubled soul"; even at Richard's castle, when the village schoolmaster does his best to crack the voices of the children who assist him, and whom he teaches, pitching the tune so high that, were I to stand on tiptoe, I could never attain to the highest note — even he, I say, gives us part of a hymn at the opening of the service. Sitting in the great transept, out of sight and hearing of most of the congregation, and often with only one of the children with me, I do often lend my voice in this first hymn as a soprano, but it is more than that delicate organ can bear, so in the two psalms I have to take the subordinate part of contralto; their collection of music being limited to the Sicilian Hymn and another equally familiar, I manage to make a tolerable second, only stopping when they put in twists and turns too numerous for my musical knowledge. I find at Ludlow most of the hymns and chants are quite familiar to me, and I fancy that the music is altogether better than one hears in country towns in England, except, of course, where there are cathedrals. At Lady Harriet Clive's school at Bromfield, the children are trained by the clerk to sing in church; that is, to chant the Gloria Patri and sing the hymn and psalms. They say it is admirably done. In the little parish churches, if the children do not sing, there is no music at all.

You are quite right with regard to English music in private — it is both old-fashioned and tasteless. Every one plays, too, the same things, for English music is very expensive, and if a young lady gets a new piece, it goes all around the neighborhood and is copied by each of her friends successively. Miss Beale plays in a more modern style than any one I have heard, but yet without taste. Miss R. has an admirable touch and plays well, with a good execution, but her music are pieces with variations, long-winded marches, and such things. You say truly I have heard nobody like M. A. My cousin, K. F., plays remarkably well for a girl, and gives promise of being a finished performer.

Before I leave the subject of music, let me do greater justice than I have done to the Ludlow organ. I have just come from the church, the full-

ness and roundness of its tones are still fresh in my
ear. It needs, it seems to me, only our

> "Timotheus,[1] placed on high
> Amid the tuneful quire"

to make it quite perfect. In truth, my dear J., it is
not so much any want of excellence in the instrument I miss, as it is your own masterly hand to
awaken its slumbering powers. I am quite sure
that you would find in your possession the master
key to unlock treasures hitherto undreamed of.

Don't think that, because English women are
not musical, they are uninteresting and charmless.
I know your old prejudice: an English woman, in
your opinion, is a combination of dowdy flounces
and ill-assorted colors, a large waist and red face.
With Miss W. for your last experience, it is not surprising that your opinion should be exaggerated.
Ah, my dear J., if you could see Miss Clive, Lady
Harriet Herbert, I could not answer for your long
retaining possession of that neglected and recently
discovered organ (what shall I call it?) — a heart?
I confess that they have not the beauty of Americans nor the natural grace of French women, nor
the taste in dress of both, but the high-born English
woman is something quite perfect — elegant, highbred, affable, warm-hearted, simple, unaffected,
and accomplished and cultivated to a degree we
rarely see. We are so fortunate in our family as
to have women equal in many respects to them.

[1] Dryden, *Alexander's Feast.*

Neither the Countess of Powis, daughter of a Duke and the descendant of a long line of illustrious Montroses, nor Lady Harriet Clive, equally distinguished, is more elegant in my eyes, or more highbred in manners and appearance than are they. Though they are both handsome women, Aunt M.[1] is handsomer.

If there is one thing more than another that has charmed me in the English that I have seen, it is their manners in their own family, the attention and respect with which each treats the other, the graceful courtesy which displays itself in the most trivial actions, and the profound respect which children accord to their parents. I have learned to deprecate in the strongest manner the baneful effects of the disregard which is paid to these things in America, and I trust I may profit by it.

Through the papers we have terrible accounts of the cold weather that you are having; for the last three days we have had clear, cold weather, cold only on comparison with what we have had. We had a slight snowstorm which has covered the Clee Hills and the Brown Clee, just enough to produce a slightly clouded sky which overhangs them, a beautiful effect. I have worn my cloak twice since I have been here; I never have used my muff and my tippet — only occasionally. The white frost which covers the ground with the most delicate raiment is much dreaded, as if it were the signal for a freezing

[1] Mrs. Henry Hills.

up of everything. The only ice we have had was before Christmas, which proves the truth of a proverb Mr. Charlton told us, that if there is ice enough to bear a goose before Christmas, there will not be ice enough to bear a chick after Christmas.

Your account of the performances at Miss K.'s was very entertaining and something quite novel. I told Miss Clive of them in return for an account she gave me of some theatricals she had witnessed at Lord Delimere's, at which "Whittington and his Cat" were played. We thought, however, that yours must be even more entertaining.

I went on Wednesday to a meeting for the advancement of schools, at which the Bishop of this diocese presided, but time does not permit me to tell you about it, and if you feel sufficiently interested in church matters, my letter to H. next week will tell you all about it.

XI

MY DEAR H——:

So little of interest has occurred since I sent J.'s letter and yours that I am running the risk of again being stupid by sending by this steamer. I feared it would not be entertaining to describe long walks that give me great pleasure, in which the only incident might be the sight of a new cottage or a glimpse of the Vignyles or the Clee Hills or Mary Knoll under a new point of view. Nor, I am afraid, could I make anything more out of a ride that I enjoy more than I can express, in which a ditch was not jumped nor a hedge taken. If I am not to draw upon my imagination for my facts, you must be content with a description of a public meeting which we attended last week, and one or two little incidents.

This meeting was held in the ballroom at Ludlow and was for the purpose of advancing education among the poor. The Bishop of Hereford presided and Mr. Clive and the Earl of Powis were among the principal speakers. I felt as if I must be reading a newspaper report. Imagine the magnificent effect of "the noble Earl" and "My Lord Bishop" and other high-sounding terms. I confess it did not offend my republican ears at all; on the contrary,

I found that my flagging attention was always aroused by these sonorous words.

As we drove up, we encountered the yellow coach and four of Lady Harriet with postillions, the carriage of the Earl and Mr. Clive's dogcart. The Clive party were the only persons in the room when we entered, which gave us a pleasant little chat before others came. Lady Harriet arranged with us to sit with them, which made it very pleasant.

The Bishop was a little man in breeches and gaiters and silk apron. The meeting was opened with prayer by the Bishop, who, by the by, is Dr. Hampden, whose letters of controversy with the Bishop of Exeter have given him a name. He is a very low churchman, and a very uninteresting speaker, and I was very glad when he gave way to the Reverend Mr. Evans, who made his report as Secretary of the Archdeanery at Hereford.

These schools are on church principles and have been established in other dioceses where they have gone to a great expense in building houses and having training schools for teachers, and otherwise doing things more expensively than this diocese could afford. The Archdeanery of Hereford, however, in a more humble way has been very successful in pursuing this plan, and the object of the meeting was to promote the cause in the Archdeanery of Salop and to raise funds for the purpose. The whole plan is very sensible. They have organizing masters who travel about and visit the schools, improving the methods of instruction, and during the four weeks of harvest, when the children go into the fields, they have a training school for the teachers, which is productive of great good, establishing a system and order which nothing else could give.

Mr. Clive is the most prosy, diffuse, and uninteresting speaker I ever heard. I felt sorry for Lady Harriet. The Earl of Powis is considered a very clever man. Last year, they say, on the occasion of a meeting against the Papal aggression, he made a very fine speech. He was accused of being very high church and, I suppose, of sympathizing with the Papal movement, and he came out in a very sarcastic and able defence. His style was in the highest degree elegant and gentlemanly, but every word told, particularly as the Bishop of Hereford was in charge. On this occasion, he spoke most sensibly and fluently, in spite of that occasional hesitation so fashionable among the *haut ton*. Still, such perfect unanimity prevailed that there was nothing to bring him out in the style in which they say he particularly excels. Besides, the audience was cold and the room still colder, and, as he said, when he stood by Richard and myself, at lunch, "It requires a good deal of artificial choleric to produce a reaction." He appears to be very pleasant with no pretension. I assure you, I talked to him with much more ease than I would to a New York beau.

Several other speakers followed, but no new facts were elicited, and had it not been, as I said before, for the magic words of "the noble Earl" and "My Lord," I should have lost entirely the two last speakers. As it was, Miss Mary Clive and I indulged in many whispers, for I was to see her for the last time, as she must leave Oakly Park the next day to take care of her invalid aunt, the Duchess of Northumberland.

Aunt Catherine and Maria were introduced by Lady Harriet to the Bishop. We went to lunch about four o'clock, at Mr. Phillips's, the rector's, where were the Bishop and any quantity of clergymen. I am glad to have attended this meeting, for I was beginning to feel that there was nothing like an active spirit of doing good among the clergy. Still, I believe that the vitality of the Church is in the laity. Neglected by her priests, her noble teachings bear fruit in her children. The power for good in the Church is shown in that the unworthiness of her ministers in no wise diminishes the zeal of the laity. I believe that, as a people, the English are the most devout and religious in the world, while, at the same time, they are free from superstition and spiritual tyranny.

Since beginning my letter this morning, the mailbag, bearing an unusual bulky appearance, was brought in and I was happy to find your letter. By the time this reaches you, you will have become quite familiar with our distinguished and agreeable circle. Aunt C. must be loved wherever she is known. Besides being most elegant and agreeable, she is so thoroughly amiable, so interesting in every way, that she makes warm friends wherever she goes. Uncle R., too, is fully appreciated here; he is so much the man of the world, accomplished in all manly sports, so necessary here, besides possessing all the advantages of a highly cultivated and travelled experience. Thus, whoever calls has followed up the acquaintance in the most complimentary manner. Sir William and the Misses Boughton and Madame Eichbaum called the other day, but, as I was just going out riding, I did not see them. However, he left for Maria and myself a little block of limestone from his quarry for each, on the bottom of which was written thus:

Maria's was in Italian.

I send you two valentines written by Maria, as you see, one to Miss Clive which is sweet and the other to Kitty. Miss Clive immediately suspected whence it came and the next post brought a note in which the "Mortal Maid of Oakly Park" acknowledged the compliment, but protests she is personified prose. By the same post came a note from Lady Harriet telling Aunt C. that she might expect her after lunch. However, to go on about the valentines: you will observe in Kitty's the line, "Where lions, bears, and tigers are." This requires an explanation. Some time ago, Maria was talking to George Landon about there being no game preserves in America; the consequence was that game had almost disappeared from the thickly inhabited portions of America, as New England, for example, so that, when gentlemen wanted shooting, they had to go to the less populated portions, as Maine or the West.

George thought it must be very fine, but he said that he would have some hesitation in going to Maine or the West, for he thought it would be uncommonly unpleasant to stumble upon a lion. Maria allowed him to retain this scanty consolation against unlimited liberty of preserves. I dare say he would object to fishing in the Mississippi for fear of catching a whale. It is great fun to get these young men beyond their depth. However, that is neither here nor there, and has nothing to do with valentines, has it? I find myself rather discursive in my style. The custom is kept here, to a certain extent, of sending valentines, and, as Miss Clive said, "She knew no one in this neighborhood could have written hers but Maria." We amused ourselves by sending some to the Landons. Richard was a little bit magnificent that day and did not enter heartily into the fun until it was almost over.

Lady Harriet and Miss Clive paid their promised

visit on Monday, and a charming visit it was. Miss Clive was very much pleased with my illuminations and took home some of my letters to copy. In return, she is to send me a book full of handsome lettering. Miss Clive was six or seven years in illuminating a history of Ludlow, written by her father. She knows the secret of the raised and polished gold of the ancients, and she is to teach me the next time we go to Oakly Park, which will probably be next week. Lady Harriet gave me some charming bits of Court experience, for she was Bedchamber woman to the Queen for three years, but I must reserve that for when I come home.

I am afraid that I write so much, that, when I come home, I shall appear quite dull and uninteresting. The charming "Sans Varier," or Mr. Charlton, in other words, has gone to Worcester for some five or six weeks' hunting. He found it very hard to part with Aunt C., for whom he has formed a very strong friendship. "Sans Varier" is his motto, and so we make a sobriquet of it, and Maria speaks almost as tenderly of him as she does of the lost Colomb.

Our domestic circle has been enlarged and enlivened by the recent acquisition of an orphan rabbit, wounded by a ferret and of tender age, which now receives the unremitting care and tenderness of Uncle Richard, Maria, and Kitty. It had not been weaned when it found itself torn from its mother and burrow. At first, the greatest difficulty was found in inducing it to take any nourishment. A quill, forced into its mouth and filled with milk, was tried, and so unsuccessfully that the greatest trepidation was felt lest the next morning should find him a corpse. However, he did survive and is now fast growing in strength and beauty.

The milk pipe, the tenderest cabbage and lettuce that the garden affords, is furnished him with a lump of sugar for dessert. Uncle R. sits and nurses him in the most fatherly manner in the evening and resigns him to Maria only when it is time to go to bed, when Maria's vocation comes into full play. His bed is by her side, and after she has soothed him by walking up and down the room, carefully wrapped in a little blanket, he is finally composed to sleep and comfortably covered up. There are times when he is restless, and then Maria has to take him into bed with her until he is quiet. Early rising is evidently a virtue early instilled into him, but consideration for others has never been culti- vated, so that Maria is frequently aroused early in the morning by his scratching and scrambling to get out, or else there lingers in him a vulgar taste for digging with his little paws. I am sorry to say that my impression is that, notwithstanding the good society into which he has been introduced and his comfortable home, he would prefer his "Hail fellow, well met" among his own race, and his native burrow.

I am so happy that you are in New York, and it would make me unhappy that you should be having a stupid time while I enjoy so much. I feel that this is the happiest part of my life. Most happiness is, in a great measure, the result of excitement. Here, that does not produce any portion of my enjoyment, and I have time to know how happy I am and, as I told you before, to feel that I satisfy two visions, the physical for the present and the mental for the future. While most of the family have gone through a sort of acclimating, I have done nothing but grow fat. I am amused at my own feeling of conscious superiority when persons are talked of as being very thin. Richard told me the other day that I was really getting a double chin.

XII

MY DEAR H——:

Uncle Richard unexpectedly told us a few days ago
that he should leave this morning for Liverpool.
As yet Aunt Catherine knows nothing about it, and
so much does he dread to tell her, that I doubt if he
goes for another week. In the meantime it be-
hooves me to be prepared, and I am sorry to have
so little to send, particularly in drawings; it has
been too damp and cold to sketch out of doors, so
I can only send you two sketches; that of the church
at Richard's castle, taken on Monday, one of the
loveliest days which we have had. It is not the side
by which you enter, nor does it give you the sepa-
ration between the chancel and the tower, but I
meant, of course, to have drawn the other side. I
found my time fully occupied by my perspective,
windows, etc.

Maria took the other side, but it is so much out
of drawing that I tried in vain to make anything
out of it. I should have gone back most willingly
to sketch it myself, but Uncle Richard thought it
exceedingly imprudent, so I had to give up my
plan. We have had three most lovely days in succession. We got home on Monday from our sketch-

ing, just in time for lunch, and immediately as we got through, R. and I went to ride and returned only in time to dress for dinner.

Then yesterday morning, soon after breakfast, R., Aunt C., and I went off to the meet of the Salway harriers, where we found ourselves the first arrivals. Aunt C. rode Romeo and I the mare, Juliet. I did not, consequently, attempt to follow, for she is young and weak. Richard was beautifully mounted; the hunter, Consul, I think, is as handsome a horse as I have seen here and R. has an elegant seat.

We saw the hare go off, but only caught a glimpse of an uncommonly good run. Aunt C. and I rode quietly through the fields and, at last, met Richard on the road. He went with us to where he supposed the hare might be, but we soon met the gentlemen returning, for Pussy had got into covert, and it is not lawful for harriers to go into covert — that is left for fox-hounds. We accompanied the gentlemen to find another hare. We sat up on the top of a hill and the hounds spread themselves over an adjoining field. They soon started a hare. She passed within a few feet of Richard and myself and got far in advance before the hounds set off in pursuit. Richard cried, "Tallyho," and I felt very much inclined to join him.

I must break off abruptly in my account of our hunt. Suffice it to say that they did not kill and we got home at two o'clock. Uncle R. announced publicly, this morning, that he should leave to-morrow, contrary to my expectations, so I have been terribly hurried to-day. I determined to make as good a drawing out of Maria's sketch as I could, and I think I succeeded. I am only sorry I have no good view of the house. I have been intending to take one, but there has always been so much to do to distract one, and Uncle Richard's final determination was so sudden that I hardly had time to write this letter. I hope, now that the weather is drier, I shall sketch a good deal.

Uncle R. will try and stop at N.H. [New Haven], but important business hurries him on to Boston. I counted upon sending you all some little remembrance, and the children in particular, but I have had no opportunity of going to Ludlow.

A note came this afternoon from Sir William Boughton, asking us to go over Tuesday at two or three o'clock, to walk about, then to drive; again on Wednesday, but only for dinner. It is very evident that an impression has been made somewhere. I fancy it is Sir William for Aunt C.

I trust to write you a more interesting letter another time. Of late, I have been so busy, what with copying from Miss Clive's book and riding and walking the rest of the time, and working R. a pair of slippers, as a birthday present. You can fancy how sleepy I get over a game of chess in the evening, so sleepy I cannot tell a knight from a bishop or a castle from a queen. Now and then R. takes an active part in gaping, and, as a general thing, I am sorry to say, I perform solo. Nothing makes me more sleepy than chess, and then I am always furnished with an excuse when I am beaten.

I don't know what to say about sending me any dresses. It would be hardly worth while to trouble Uncle R., but a fresh dress would be a comfort.

Miss B. is coming to pass a few days here next week. I am writing you on Thursday morning, before breakfast, and in haste.

XIII

MY DEAR H——:

At last I have five minutes to devote to you. I have this moment taken off my habit, which I had on at least six or seven hours to-day, and have dressed for dinner. Aunt C. and I went with Richard to the meet of Mr. Caldwell's harriers at Bemington and near Miss Beale's. Having loitered about until they found and the hare went away, we went to Miss Beale's for lunch. There we remained until three o'clock, when "Sans Varier," Richard, Henry Landon, Ogle, and Mr. Keville-Davis came in to get a glass of ale and a piece of bread and butter.

I was thankful to return home. "Sans Varier" escorted Aunt C., which gave Richard an opportunity of telling me how the first hare went away, and it was not much of a run, because she doubled so often, and then was finally lost; but how they soon found another hare, which gave a magnificent run of thirty-five minutes without a single check. Such a tale of ditches taken, such water jumps, such timber jumps, such drops, and it all fell on such interested ears! How Ogle was left, and Davis lost his hat, and Richard and Woodhouse were with the hounds all the way and came in at the death; how Consul, Richard's noble hunter, went like a bird and never once refused; how magnificent it was, how it was something fearful, that run and those jumps. And so Richard fought his battles o'er again and I listened and wished I had been there too.

As Aunt C. and I sat upon the top of the hill, the sun shining so warmly that we suffered from the heat, we looked down upon the misty landscape. Now, we would catch a glimpse of the hunters galloping across the field and the music of the hounds in full cry was borne to us. Ah, it was something inspiring!

We have had quite a gay week of it. After Uncle R. really was gone, Aunt C. began to revive and entered with pleasure into the prospect of the two dinners at Sir William Boughton's on Tuesday and Wednesday. I told you that Miss Beale was to pay us a visit, but her housekeeper was taken ill, supposed to be dying, so she has had to give it up for the present.

I have been going on too fast and came very near forgetting our sketching at the castle with Miss Clive on Friday, and the charming visit to Oakly Park on Monday. Lady Harriet wrote over to say that Miss Clive was going to be at the castle at two o'clock and would be most happy to meet us. At the appointed time, we found Miss Clive busily at work and Lady Harriet looking over her. Soon, however, Lady H. and Aunt C. left us, the former to pay some visits, the latter to shop. I made two sketches and then we took a lovely walk and found the carriage waiting for us at the turnpike gate. We did not part without an agreement to come to Oakly Park on Monday after lunch, to see Miss Clive's great book. Since I have seen that, I have some idea of the capabilities of illuminating. Miss Clive laid before us a book as large, if not larger, than Mr. Mableson's Manuscript of the Vesper Service, and bound in wood. Printed upon fine and heavy drawing paper and containing one hundred and fifty pages, it was divided into three parts; Ludlow, under the Saxons; Ludlow, under the Normans; and Ludlow, under the Lords Presidents. The whole is the history of Ludlow up to the present time and written by herself in the style of the old Chronicles. Throughout are the most exquisite etchings in India ink and brown, and water-color paintings, all views of places where the various scenes were enacted.

In the first part, what are now ruins, she has restored to what she imagined must have been the ancient glory. The Mask of Comus is most exquisitely etched, depicting the various scenes in the play. At the end of the volume are fifty views of Ludlow in water-colors and Prout's brown, a few of them being by Lady Harriet. The illuminations are principally confined to the lettering, which is beautiful beyond description. Throughout, raised and polished gold is employed which produces a beautiful effect. Mrs. Stackhouse-Acton was the first to begin this sort of thing. Miss Clive did not show me how to apply the gold, but we are to go to Acton Scott for a night and day and Mrs. Acton has promised to teach me and give me some of the composition to be used.

While we were at Oakly Park the Countess of Powis and the Ladies Herbert arrived from Walcot, only thirteen miles from Oakly Park, for a week's visit. When the gentlemen of the family go up to Parliament, the ladies visit each other. Thus Monday passed. On Tuesday morning, I took a ride of about twelve miles with Richard, and at half-past five o'clock we were to go to Downton which is six miles from this. We found the party assembled when we arrived, all of whom, with the exception of the Cuylers and ourselves, were staying in the house. It consisted of Mrs. Acton; her sister, Mrs. Walpole; Mr. and Mrs. Keville-Davis; the Misses Rushout, two elderly maiden ladies whose brother, Captain Rushout, is M.P., heir and nephew of Lord Northwick; Mr. and Mrs. Dunn; Mr. Tom Dunn, of Bircher. Never was there such a scarcity of gentlemen. Six to fourteen ladies. Poor Madame Eichbaum had the greatest difficulty in establishing the order of precedence. Whether the two Misses Cuyler should precede the Misses Rushout, the former the daughters of a Baronet, the latter the granddaughter of a Baron, and their seniors many years, was the question. It was at last settled and the Misses Cuyler were accorded the honor and even preceded old Mrs. Dunn and Aunt Catherine. Now, Miss Clive says, this is altogether wrong and would only be done in a country neighborhood and by Sir William Boughton, who is tenacious of the honor accorded to the Baronet's daughter.

At Oakly Park Aunt C. followed the Countess of Powis. You can imagine that six gentlemen are six gentlemen, and fourteen ladies are fourteen ladies, and nothing else. Some of the ladies had to be converted into beaux, and I found myself between Frances Boughton and Constance Cuyler, both sweet girls, but particularly Constance, who is very pretty and sympathizes perfectly with me in riding and horses, besides being very cultivated and agreeable.

The dinner was very like other dinners and indeed much pleasanter than you might imagine. English women are so charming, so cultivated, so superior, as a general thing, to the men, that I hardly felt the want of the lords of creation. Mrs. Stackhouse-Acton is lovely and agreeable, but her sister, Mrs. Walpole, is absurd. The latter is a great talker and particularly prides herself upon her name and relationship to Lord Orford's family. Her daughter has just married her cousin, Mr. Walpole of the Royal Navy. After asking me a great many questions about American authors, among whom was Willis, she asked me if I could get her any autographs. I told her I could probably get her one of Willis's, at which she was very much delighted. So you must ask Aunt M. if she has any notes of his she can give me. This is the first time I have heard Willis's name mentioned, though American writers are thoroughly known and universally read. Longfellow is a great favorite — everybody talks about him, wants to know how he looks, and many other questions.

We had music during the evening and again negro melodies were entreated and sung, to the regret of Richard and Maria. We got home at about one o'clock, and the next morning, immediately after breakfast, Richard and I started off for Mr. Salway's hunt with harriers. Arrived at the Bury gates, the place for the meet, we found nobody but Mr. Salway accompanied by his hounds, as scrubby and shabby a set as you can imagine. We went into the field and the hounds soon found a cold scent, and so Richard and I rode about waiting for them to find. In the meantime, Mr. Betton joined our party, and, notwithstanding the bad scent, the frosty air, and hot sun, Richard saw that the hounds would soon find, so he and I went around through a lane, and just as we got to the gate of a field, we met the hounds on full run. Off we went over the beautiful grass field at a pace, I can assure you, would astonish you, and came up just as they had a check and lost the hare, but several minutes before Mr. Salway and Mr. Betton made their appearance.

In coming back to find another hare, and after Mr. Ogle had made a fifth, I saw Mr. Betton leading his horse over a hedge, over which Ogle and Mr. Salway had leaped. So I asked him if there were a ditch on the other side. He said, "No," and asked me, in quite a derisive tone, if I would take it. Of course, I said "Yes," and, Richard going first and I following, Romeo never refused, but took the bank and hedge without touching a thorn. Of course, I was applauded, and Richard called out to Mr. Betton, "Beat that, if you can." That evening, when I met the Landons, at Downton, I was overwhelmed with compliments and congratulations.

As for Henry, he has quite taken Charles's place. We danced delightfully together and then he admired my riding; so we talk horses and dancing. Henry Landon can talk hunting and horses by the hour and you need not say a word. He usually salutes me with, "I say now, Miss Anna Maria, did you observe that bay mare the other day," or something of the sort. It is a change from Charles, who says, "Well, then, Miss Anna Maria, how are you."

But to return to the hunt. The scent was so bad and it was so cold that Richard and I returned home at two o'clock. I lunched and took a walk with Aunt C., after which it was time to dress again for Downton. Seven o'clock found us before Sir William's hospitable door. This time there were only two less gentlemen than ladies, the same party with the exception of the Cuylers and Mrs. Stack-house-Acton and the Rushouts, and the addition of Mrs. Oakly, the daughter of Lady Trembleson of this neighborhood, who, before nine months of her widowhood have expired, will be married again. Mr. Longworth and Mr. James, and others I cannot remember, completed the party.

Madame Eichbaum could afford to give me a gentleman this time, a Mr. James, who certainly was not interesting at dinner, yet I found him very agreeable and clever afterwards. However, I sat on Sir William's right. He talked enough for a dozen, and I was frightened at my proximity to him, for his great object is to pump every one to see how little they know and show how much he knows. I got along very well until he asked me what would be the effect of all the California gold upon the circulation, and I had to confess that I had not given the subject much thought. I must admit that I think Sir William a humbug and a great tyrant.

With the exception of the Misses Boughton, those poor girls, for there are five, are like frightened fawns. To all one's remarks they say, "Oh, really," and in such a way that it is not at all suggestive and does not in the least assist you in carrying on a conversation. There is no end of the "Ohs" and "Ahs" with which people mark their attention and interest.

We Americans, you know, say, "Yes, Yes."

What with the riding and the champagne and the comfortable seat in the chimney corner, I found myself nearly asleep when the ladies went upstairs except Mrs. Keville-Davis, Frances Boughton, and Theresa by my side. If I did arouse myself from my dreamy state and address a remark to the latter, she would start and look wild and say, "Oh, really," and Mrs. Keville-Davis, every now and then, in a low tone, said something to Frances Boughton about dress and she would say, "Oh, really," and I should soon have gone to sleep with this lullaby of "Oh, really," if the ladies had not returned and the Cuylers and Landons arrived for the evening, and if the gentlemen had not left their wine in the dining-room.

I soon found myself wide awake as Henry Landon and I went flying around the polished floor of the dining-room to the music of a lively waltz. It was, however, rather a slow evening, notwithstanding the fact that I danced all the time. Between one and two o'clock supper was announced and we found two libraries open, two tables in one and one in the other. Thus we formed parties and seated ourselves. My lot fell among the Landons with Mr. James and Madame Eichbaum at the foot of the table. Here, Mr. James's cleverness came out, for, having thoroughly discussed the viands placed before us, we drew up towards Mr. James and began telling ghost stories. I soon found, however, that my immediate neighbors had spirits of their own,

too talkative and noisy to court those already laid
in the vasty deep. So I seated myself on a cushion
by Madame Eichbaum, and here such harrowing
stories were told, such ghosts called up, as would
have startled the beard of the Weird Sisters out of a
week's growth.

After supper we had a little more dancing, and
about half-past three we were glad to find ourselves
at home.

On Friday the party from Oakly Park promised
to come to lunch and take a walk with us on the
Vignyles, but Lady Harriet wrote over to say that
Lady Lucy and Lady Harriet Herbert had such bad
colds that the walk would be impossible, but they
would come after lunch.

It would be impossible to describe to you Shaw's
(the butler's) gratification when the yellow coach
and four, with postillions and footman, drew up
before the door, or depict to you the smile of mingled pride and pleasure with which he announced
"Lady 'Aryet Clive, Miss Clive, and the Countess
of Powis and Lady 'Aryet 'Erbert." It is too funny
to see the bland smile which his otherwise austere
face assumes when he pronounces a great name. I,
myself, was once witness to his reception of Sir
William's coachman in the stable, and it was in the
highest degree gracious and cordial. Indeed, it was
only equalled by the *empressement* with which he
requested to put me on the pony.

We had a charming visit. Lady Powis is less

stately than Lady Harriet and a most charming person. As for Miss Clive, she is everything that is lovely and amiable. She is making a drawing apiece for Maria and me. Miss Clive asked me whether Aunt C. had any idea of being presented at Court; she said that they had been talking of it and were particularly anxious that we should have such an opportunity of seeing so great a spectacle of English society, and much more to the same purpose. This, of course, is *entre nous*. The idea, thus presented, was not agreeable to Aunt C., but whether it will be or not, it is impossible to say. It is very evident that, if we do go to London, or when we do go, the Clives will be as kind as they have been here.

The Misses Rushout, when they called the other day, gave their address in London and begged Aunt C., when she came to town, to let them know, that they would like to show us the picture galleries. Besides, they should speak to Lord Northwick that, in case we came to Lemington, we might have peculiar privileges in seeing his fine collection of pictures, one of the best in England. Thus everybody is kind to the most flattering degree. Sir William told me that the whole neighborhood would sign a petition to Uncle Richard not to leave the Moor.

In consequence of my association with aristocratic personages I have learned to pronounce your name in a new way, and for the future, when I call you "Haryet," you will know I wish to be particularly elegant. "Haryet" is aristocratic — Harriet is vulgar. It gives too much importance to the "R." Hence, on great occasions I shall say, "Dear Haryet," and if anybody questions my pronunciation, I shall say, "It was thus, Madam, that the Countess of Powis addressed her daughter of like name."

Here I am, almost at the end of my fourth sheet, without saying one word about the letter I received last Thursday which gave me so much pleasure.

Have you seen anything of Fanny Bloodgood and the Leavinworths and Kings?

Richard has just put his head in at the door to say he is going to order the horses. I go, on Tuesday, to Mr. Wickstead's meet of harriers, about nine miles from this. Constance Cuyler is to be there. I was weighed yesterday in my habit and weighed nine stone two, one hundred and twenty-eight pounds. The new habit comes home to-night.

XIV

MY DEAR MOTHER:

I know no reason why H. should monopolize my valuable correspondence to the exclusion of yourself. If you knew how much pleasure your letters give me, you would have begun to write me a long time ago. Since I last wrote, Miss Beale has been added to our circle; a most charming acquisition, she has proved. She is very lively, accomplished, and undeniably agreeable, always ready to amuse or be amused. She studies German with us in the morning. In German I am getting along very well. I hear so much spoken about me that the pronunciation is not difficult to get, nor, as yet, have I found any insurmountable difficulties.

Yesterday morning I got up at seven o'clock to learn my lesson. At quarter to ten, behold me, equipped in my new habit, for the hunt at Bitterly. And how, you ask, does the new habit look? how is it made? does it fit well? All these questions I know follow so quickly that I will crowd them all into one sentence. Aunt C. says it fits well, Richard says it looks particularly becoming both to face and figure. It is half bloomer; that is, a white waistcoat, buttoned to the throat with a tight jacket and short skirt and two buttons in front. I attracted an immense deal of admiration at Bitterly, not only from my admiring cousin, but from all the gentlemen of the hunt by my bold and graceful riding, and the correctness of my costume (so Richard says).

Richard's horse is unfortunately lame, so he rode a pony. We were, therefore, unable to go quite in front, but we showed quite half the field the trick. I don't think I shall ever forget yesterday. Most unfortunately, Consul was lame and when we got into Ludlow, we found that the coachman had been able to get a choice between a mare that was stone blind so that the eyes were perfectly white, or a horse that was dead lame. Having eyes himself, Richard preferred the blind animal to the halt.

Thus we set off to join Sir Charles Cuyler and Constance at Henley. Arrived at Henley, we found them waiting for us. We took our line of march immediately for the fields that were to be drawn, and we reached the appointed place at the very moment that Mr. Wickstead and his exquisite pack, followed by twenty or thirty men well mounted, came up. There is no finer pack of harriers in England; they are of such equal size, thirteen inches high, that the backs of the whole eleven couples and a half, standing in a line, would present a perfectly even surface. Then they are as like as peas, so that, having seen one, you have seen all. They work beautifully and obey the voice of the master as pointers would. No sooner were they turned into the field than they found, and away went the hare and so did we.

In the meantime, Mr. O., the rector of Bitterly, offered Richard his pony and, while Richard went to get it, I remained with Sir Charles. We had a most exciting run and were in at the death. You can imagine nothing finer than this beautiful pack going off in chase and in full cry and the field of finely mounted men following on the gallop. In truth, I was so excited I have not at all a clear recollection of it. Richard arrived just before the death, so that he was with me all the time in the second run, during most of which I was parted from Sir Charles and Constance, and, while they remained in the lane, I followed with Richard. Again we got in at the death, which to me is one of the prettiest scenes. All the dogs are collected around their master, while he holds up the hare before them, and recounts the run, praising each one, as it deserves, and calling each one affectionately by name. The gentlemen stand grouped around and some dismount, while others assume a reposing posture and talk over the hedges taken, etc., etc. Now it is that we have an opportunity of examining their fine horses, and an English thoroughbred hunter is a most beautiful animal, the long neck is so fine; and then Englishmen ride so well. As a general thing, their seat is so different from the American's. I always studied Richard's seat especially and all good seats in general, that I might be able to teach W.[1]

Constance Cuyler rides wonderfully well. Her horse is only four years old and very high-spirited and he jumped and reared and kicked and did everything but get her off. She managed him wonderfully well. Richard says that with a third horn I could do as well, but I doubt it. There is so much in the practice of the fingers. Sir Charles was so kind as to give me some instruction both as regards the reins and my seat, but of the latter, Richard did not approve. We left at half-past two o'clock, for Consul cast a shoe, to lunch at Henley and Aunt C. took leave with Miss Beale before we left the dining-room. At five o'clock I was again on my way home, having been on horseback six hours and ridden twenty miles, for it was fourteen miles to the meet and back. Do you not think that was a pretty good day? You can imagine that my strength has increased when I tell you that I was not stiff after it, and only tired enough to be sleepy during the evening, like all hunting people.

Sir Charles gave some incidents of his stay in New York in which Mrs. Douglas Cruger figured in a very absurd light. There is nobody who relishes a good story so much as the little Baronet. He has a thick blank book in which he pastes anecdotes that he cuts out of papers and all sorts of queer things and odd sayings, and as for conundrums, there is no

[1] William Gaston Fay, her brother.

end to his collection of them. I remember the first day he dined here, he gave us one that is very good: "If a pig should wish to build a house, what would be the first thing which he would do?" You give it up, of course. He would tie a knot in his tail and say, 'Here is a pig's tie for you.'"

Sunday, March 21st

I RECEIVED H.'s letter this morning, which, as you can imagine, I was most happy to get, particularly as it tells me that she is enjoying herself. It is cruel of her to thrust her pretty dresses in my face, for I am getting as shabby as possible. Miss Heighington cut my habit very well, but I don't at all like the idea of her making a nice dress; and, even if I were willing to trust her, I should not care to buy a dress in Ludlow, our plans are so undecided, even if you would let me. It seems uncertain whether we shall go to Paris, London seems tolerably certain, and Aunt C. thinks she will go in May and, when Uncle R. returns, something will be determined upon.

Since March began, we have not had one drop of rain. Most of the time it has been clear, and if an east wind has occasionally annoyed us, it is not to be compared to ours. Yesterday, I suffered with the heat in riding, and Aunt C. and myself sat out in the open air in the afternoon and I read to her while she sewed. This morning I was dressed about half-past seven, sitting out on the steps of the conservatory. I have been sitting all the morning with the windows open. The buds of the trees and hedges are coming out, the banks are covered with primroses under the hedges, while sweet-scented violets, white, blue, and pink, can be picked in quantities. Periwinkles hang over the banks and mingle with the primroses. The meadows are getting trim with daisies pied. There are buttercups enough and to spare to test under the chin every day the love of one's friends for butter, and wild strawberries are in bloom. The peaches in the hothouse are as large as wild plums, and daffodils and heather fill the beds always here in the form of a palm-leaf. Everything bespeaks the opening of spring. I write to the running accompaniment of singing birds, interrupted often and rendered inharmonious by the monotonous cawing of the rooks who are busy building their nests and keep up a constant scolding and cawing not at all pleasant. How much you would enjoy this English climate. How it can have been so vilified, I cannot understand. It seems to me there is more to enjoy in England than in any part of the world. There is no extreme cold or heat. One has, to be sure, gloomy days, when fog wraps everything in an impenetrable cloud, but it is no raw, chilling fog. On the contrary, it is kindly. It refreshes one, too, and softens the skin, and when the sun does break through it, one greets him with so much pleasure. Then, naturally, it is so beautiful — the mistiness of the atmosphere tones down all rough points, all garish lights and glaring tints. All Nature is so harmonious and subdued — I have heard but two discordant sounds, one the croaking of the rooks, the other the hooting of the owls. Every night, some unhappy owl doth to the moon complain in such shrill and dolorous accents that I am quite sure the raven down of darkness has all been turned the wrong way.

Thursday

I HAVE this moment got through my German lesson and have just been for the mail-bag to finish this. Tuesday Richard and I rode to Ludlow in the afternoon, and, in coming away, met Sir Charles and Constance and Mr. and Mrs. Betton, when we joined the party and had a charming ride with them to Henley, notwithstanding the fact that we would only have half an hour to get home in and to dress for dinner, at quarter to seven o'clock. As I rode the carriage mare, we found no difficulty in accomplishing the distance and being ready for dinner. We had a charming ride, and Sir Charles, as usual, was very funny and agreeable.

The Clives have all gone to Hewell Grange in Worcestershire, Lady Harriet's other place. After Easter, they leave for London. Miss Clive and Victoria, with the German governess, lunched here last Thursday and took a walk up to the Vignyles. We miss them, for, although we did not see them very often, there was almost every day a note either from Miss Clive or Lady Harriet.

XV

I was this morning so happy as to receive your letter and my mother's, for which I had been anxiously watching. You make me quite envious of your charming admirers, but how can you be so unkind as to conceal the name of the one *par excellence;* and to apologize, too, for writing too much about yourself is the unkindest cut of all; as if I had not a right to know and a wish to hear everything, however minute, that concerns you. It is not, however, worth while to scold. Scoldings, like sentiments, "should be served hot," and a voyage across the Atlantic would deprive either dish of a great deal of choleric.

I am quite at a loss what to write to you about. I cannot write of a variety of beaux. The Landons have been for some time effectually alienated. Ned, out of whom I might have made something, retired from the field early in the season, and Charles is altogether too stupid. I relaxed long ago in my efforts to fascinate him. The hunting season is off and Henry's horse is lame, so the subjects of conversation with him are pretty nearly exhausted. I have talked to him most vigorously as long as his horse had the grease, but lameness, somehow or other, does not interest me much. Ogle is exceedingly clever, in spite of his rudeness and radicalism and his sweeping sarcasms. What retorts you and he would have! Indeed, to such a pitch has the want of incident in our daily life arrived, that Maria cannot be sufficiently thankful to any one who will give her a new name to find out in the Book of the Peerage. I am afraid Maria is in an incipient stage of tuft-hunting. She has studied the Peerage until she is as familiar with the defunct ancestors of the present aristocracy as any grave-digger and as good as a parish register in respect to births and marriages.

German occupies a great deal of my time. I take a lesson every morning, which always consists of two or three readings, exercises in Ollendorff which must be repeated in addition to any rules or observations that may occur, and a verb and translation. Richard is as strict as any school master. If my grammar lesson is not perfect, I have it the next day, and in addition to it a new one. Thus, in order to draw a little, I have to get up at half-past six o'clock in the morning.

I have not attempted to add archery to my other occupations. While the rest of the universe has been travelling at its customary rate, through its orbit, the Moor Park has remained stationary under the sign of Sagittarius. The rage for bows and arrows has prevailed to an alarming extent. Richard has got to shooting exceedingly well, but I entreat him to confine his darts to the target and pretend to feel an occasional stab, all of which he does not like at all, and puts on a magnificent air, says in a severe tone, "Annie, Annie."

It is the fashion in England for archery, and the ladies and gentlemen practice a great deal. In summer, they have archery meetings at which prizes are adjudged. Miss Clive adds this to her other accomplishments, and has won among other things a beautiful chatelaine and watch. While she is at Oakly Park, she draws untiringly, but at Hewell Grange drawing is laid aside and archery takes its place.

We have terrible accounts of the weather in America, while here, with the exception of an occasional east wind, nothing can be finer. They say that the change in the English climate is owing to the immense amount of draining that is going on. Indeed, it is so dry that farmers are complaining, and yesterday Richard and I had to leave the turnpike, so dusty was it; but of course, for the better, as we gave ourselves up to following any path we happened to like, and the consequence was that we had an exquisite ride through a country I have not seen before, but quite as beautiful as this.

Wednesday, April 7th

THE even tenor of our daily life has been interrupted by a visit of Colonel Cecil Forrester, an old friend of Uncle Richard's and Aunt Catherine's, whom they knew when he was stationed with his regiment in Canada. He was here last autumn, passing through England on his way from Paris to Dublin. He wrote from London that he should come on Monday. Nevertheless, he arrived unexpectedly before dinner, and if he were not the most reserved of men, he would have told us, I am sure, that a most cheerful scene greeted him as he crossed the park on foot, having left his baggage at the turnpike gate. Richard and the governess, Kitty Fay and Kitty Landon were shooting at the target in the park in front of the house. Aunt C. sat near them, in a Bath-chair, talking to Janet Landon, Maria, Mrs. Landon, and I stood near the house, talking to Mr. and Mrs. Betton, who were on horseback, while Ogle and Henry Landon, having got through their game of billiards in the hall, joined us, as the Colonel's tall figure was recognized by Willie and Lily with cries of "Colonel Forrester, Colonel Forrester." I did not see him until we met in the drawing-room just before dinner. The Colonel is tall and dark and altogether very military-looking. I should think he must be between forty-five and fifty. He is very agreeable, notwithstanding an impenetrable reserve which defies all efforts at removal. He leaves to-day to our great regret. He has been in America several times, and so early as 1827.

Aunt C. had letters for the second time yesterday from Uncle R. He seems to enjoy himself very much, and does not speak, as yet, of coming home.

He is struck with the unfinished aspect of everything in America and the want of the order and universal good taste which prevails here in domestic arrangements. People congratulate him upon his rejuvenation, and he certainly looks very well and very handsome. The weather must be something quite dreadful, but the fields and banks here are full of bright flowers and spring appears to advance very rapidly. They say it is seldom that the trees are fairly out before the last of May or the first of June.

There is to be a ball on the 23rd at Ludlow, given by the railroad company upon the opening of the railroad from Shrewsbury, a most important event in the annals of Ludlow, though I fancy that "Mr. Weller," of the Red Rover Coach, may be of a contrary opinion. On the morning of the day, there are to be all sorts of sports in the castle yard and a champagne breakfast, and, in the evening, there will be a ball to which every one will go, navvies (workmen) and all. Sir Charles Cuyler and Sir William Boughton have put down their names, though it took Sir Charles a long time to decide about it. This is a funny country, is it not, when people, otherwise so exclusive, go to a mixed ball, while we in America would scorn to appear before the common herd décolletée and otherwise dressed to the best possible advantage. It is still doubtful whether we shall go. Richard is very anxious for it.

There was so little of interest to tell you that I did not begin my letter early as I should do, in order to give time for something interesting to happen, but to no effect, as you see.

XVI

I LITTLE imagined last year that I should be writing
you on Easter Day in England, and a most lovely
day it is. The sky is clear, the air is soft and balmy,
the fields are full of daisies, the banks are covered
with primroses and violets and the hedges and
trees are hastening to put on their spring dress.
There is something peculiarly tranquil about English Sundays. I am always reminded of a line in
Gray's Elegy, "And all the air a solemn stillness
holds." Indeed, Richard and I never cease to be
impressed with the poetical associations which
throng around the scenery. When I write you of
primroses and violets on the banks and daisies and
daffodils in the fields, I almost imagine myself
writing in numbers. In my fancy, the landscape
seems, as it were, surrounded by a laurel wreath.
The air must be vocal with the tuneful lyres of
those who have so often sung the manifold charms
of this lovely country, for I never go out and never
look at a scene which does not suggest some line or
other of verse that I have known.

Good Friday afternoon was as lovely as to-day,
and we enjoyed it to the fullest extent, by going to
walk, Richard, Maria, Kitty, and I and the govern-

ess wandering along through the fields, while Richard made willow whistles for us, which, when they were completed, we all blew at once. As we approached the house on our return home, Aunt C. was sitting on the doorsteps, and marshalled in battle array, with Richard preceding, we saluted her as well as we could for laughing and a full blast of whistles, "aggravating our voices" as Nicholas Bottom would say, and whistling until the echo was hoarse and would not answer. Was not this an intellectual amusement?

To-day the mail-bag brought Aunt C. a letter addressed in an unknown hand and sealed with a coronet. To open it, to read it, to find it signed "Powis," was the work of only a few moments, but not so the pleasure it was proposed to afford us. His lordship has invited us to come to Walcot, eighteen miles from this, to lunch and pass the morning any fine day after Monday. Of course, we shall go. Walcot is one of his two estates, and the other is Powis Castle in Wales.

Wednesday, April 14th

As on every other occasion, yesterday was most auspicious for our visit to Walcot. We left this at half-past nine o'clock, Kitty going with us and Richard driving on the box with the coachman. Our route took us through Bishop's Castle, where there is no castle, but, instead, afforded us a view of the ruins of Stoke Castle, of which I sent you sketches. About twelve, we found ourselves at the lodge gates. The approach was less imposing than I had expected, the avenue being nothing particular and bringing us up before a great red pile built without any regard to taste and too square and modern to be picturesque. No sooner did we draw up than the door was thrown open for us, which admitted us into a half hall and half vestibule. Another footman stood ready to usher us through folding doors, leading from this into the drawing-room and into the presence of Lady Powis and the Ladies Lucy and Haryet (Harriet) Herbert. They were seated in this fine room surrounded by portraits of their ancestors by various great artists, Reynolds and Angelica Kauffmann and others. A grand piano here, comfortable sofas there, tables covered with new and rich books, objects of art and vertu and elegance and taste and comfort pervaded the whole. Nothing could exceed the cordiality with which we were received. We were soon seated and chatting pleasantly and interrupted by the entrance of the Honorable Mr. Herbert, a youth of sixteen, and an Etonian. In a few moments Lord Powis made his appearance, having just come from examining some carbines for his yeomanry, for he is Colonel of all the yeomanry of Salop.

A walk was soon proposed, and then Lady Powis led us through a charming suite of apartments, the first of which was the morning room opening from the drawing-room and very pleasantly arranged with everything that is comfortable; but here, as everywhere else, one is particularly struck with the absence of elaborate upholstery. From this room, we entered one much larger, used as a drawing-room literally. Here was an easel and drawings in various stages, engravings, etc., in portfolios, but the interest of the room was centred in the case against the wall, filled with Indian curiosities, brought home by the great ancestor, Lord Clive. There were guns, richly ornamented in various ways, pistols, sabres and one superb scabbard and staff inlaid with jewels, and many other things I cannot remember.

Opening out of this room was the library, differing, however, very little from other libraries. Then we went out upon the terrace by the garden which was very prettily arranged and full of flowers, then on by a winding path up on a hill, where we found ourselves at an Indian bungalow, which, in deep shade and wrapt in solitude, would, it seemed to me, be cool under a burning sun. I asked Lady Harriet if it were not delightful on a warm summer afternoon and she said that she had never been at Walcot in summer and only fancied it might be. At the bungalow we changed companions, Maria taking Lord Powis from Aunt C. and Aunt C. having Lady Powis in his place and Richard changing with me, Lady Harriet for Lady Lucy, and the Etonian devoting himself to Kitty. Thus accompanied, we resumed our walk, strolling along under a magnificent avenue of splendid chestnuts; then leaving it and having fine views of beautiful Scotch pines, such as one sees in pictures; then down a shady path to the borders of an artificial lake, a mile long, where swans floated about and flapped their wings and otherwise showed their content as sensible birds should.

I found Lady Lucy very charming, exceedingly sensible and wonderfully intelligent. She inquired with great interest about the American Church, in which her interests had been awakened by a little book, written on the subject lately by one of the Wilberforces, and then we went on from one thing to another. She described to me her presentation at Court and altogether made herself most agreeable.

This charming walk at length came to an end and Lady Powis showed us upstairs to rooms prepared for us where we arranged ourselves for lunch, which was served in a fine large dining-room that one reached by a long, narrow corridor. The walls were hung with many fine pictures. When one considers that Powis Castle is on a far grander scale than Walcot, and the house in town is equally rich in works of art, one has some idea of the wealth which has procured all these treasures. The lunch was served, as is the custom, in simple style, on painted English china and all placed on the table at once, and consisted of soup for the first course, chickens, roast lamb and mint sauce, pressed beef

and cold meats on a side table, entrées of patties
and creams and jellies and rhubarb tarts. There
is nothing more fashionable here than rhubarb,
which is in color a brilliant pink.

While we were at the table, the afternoon amusements were decided upon. A riding party was to
be formed of Lord Powis, Lady Harriet, and Mr.
Herbert, and Richard. The rest of us were to go in
the carriage to see a fine camp of the ancient Brit-
ons, which crowned a hill some two miles from the
house. While the carriage was getting ready, Lady
Powis took us into the picture gallery which opened
out of the dining-room. Here the walls were covered with beautiful pictures, among them a Canaletto, a Rembrandt, a Tintoretto, and others.
Not the least curious was the full-length portrait of
an Indian Prince and a little boy, probably his son.
In a niche was a very good organ by one Green,
who might be Smith or Brown for aught John
would know of him, probably. It was arranged
with a barrel so that it could be wound up and
made to play, and for John's benefit, I add a list of
the stops: 15th, 12th, Cornet, Flute, Stopt, Diapason, Open Diapason, Sesquialtera; and I believe I
have mentioned them all. Lady Lucy played us a
great portion of one of the Mozart Masses, which
was a little too much of a good thing. The effect of
the organ was particularly good in the conservatory, which joins the gallery. Time was when Walcot was quite celebrated for its immense quantity of

glass, for the grandfather of the present Earl had such a passion for spending money without regard either to taste or utility that it has taken years to remove the mounds of earth required to make the garden and terrace. The conservatory is very large and even now filled with beautiful flowers and trees, among which I recognized some Southern friends.

Lady Harriet made her appearance for the ride, and the horses and carriage being announced, the party was broken up and the equestrians, accompanied by a groom in livery, started before us.

Lady Powis did not accompany us, so that we managed to dispose of our five selves very comfortably in the barouche with coachman on the box, whose dimensions were as great as those of an aristocratic whip should be. We drove through the noble park for about two miles, and then, there not being a carriage road any further, we left the carriage and walked the rest of the way, really suffering with the heat. We toiled up an ascent of about half a mile until we reached, with what pleasure, the pine-crowned summit of the camp. There, Kitty and I seated ourselves on a bank and, surrounded by the work of a thousand years ago, enjoyed not less the shade which only fifty years had produced, for here beautiful trees were planted by his lordship's grandfather. Lady Lucy, Aunt C., and Maria continued their walk around the camp, when Kitty and I were soon startled by the tramp of horses, and, turning, we had a most charming view of the riding party as they came on through the dark woods, and broke upon our admiring sight in the most picturesque manner. Lord Powis sought the rest of the party and, dismounting, gave his horse to the groom and walked down to the carriage with us.

The view is magnificent from this eminence. On a clear day one can see the park of Powis Castle, nineteen miles distant.

Lady Harriet's mare is a perfect beauty and she has a most graceful seat. Richard enjoyed his ride exceedingly. The gallops over the turf that the park affords are something beyond compare. By the time we got back to the house, the clock had struck six, so that the carriage was immediately ordered and we parted with many regrets and the wish on their part to meet us in London.

One of the most curious things I saw, which I ought to have mentioned, was in the morning room — a picture of small size of Lord Herbert of Cherbury, whose fifth brother was George Herbert, the poet, and whose family is the same, with the addition of more than four hundred years to its age, as Lady Powis's, for the title of Powis and the name of Herbert came through her, when her husband, Lord Clive, received the Earldom of Powis, once belonging to some branch of Lady Powis's family. In like manner, Mr. Clive hopes to be raised to the Peerage and made Lord Plymouth, a title which died with Lady Harriet Clive's brother.

We arrived home about nine o'clock, having spent the day that we shall long remember.

Wednesday, April 21st

YESTERDAY was a great day in the annals of Ludlow, the celebration of the opening of the railroad. Why the hills and the valleys did not rise up against the modern monster introduced into secluded Shropshire surprises me, and why the wonderful echo in the castle that once replied only to the din of arms and in later times gave answer to nothing less unusual than the call of the guide for the benefit of visitors — why this same echo will not expire of bronchitis, in having to give back whistle for whistle, is still more surprising.

We got in town too late to see the train arrive, but we were told that all the fields around the station were a sea of people, most of whom were as innocent of ever having seen an engine as the English would say we Americans were of ever having seen the sea serpent. We went into town under a laurel arch. The Angel's Inn was decorated with greens and flowers and the Town Hall was resplendent with verdant trimmings. At the station was another arch upon which was lettered, "Welcome to Ludlow, Success to Brassy" (the Contractor). Before the Angel's Inn, for some distance up and down the street, stood every variety of carriage, the Angel being able to admit only the horses. All sorts of people thronged the street — tall women in flounces, little women in flounces, hogshead-like proportions in flounces, pole-like proportions in flounces — as a general thing the flounces being of the heaviest material — all sorts of colors, all sorts of mantles and shawls, all sorts of bonnets, without doubt the spring fashion when Mrs. Noah had to change shop and retire from the Ark; this conglomeration of bonnets and shawls being interspersed with the masculine element in coats of every shade of gray and brown and black, and trousers no less various, smock frocks, hats and caps and wide-awakes, topping heads owning noses as red and purple as beer and port wine can make them — post-boys in yellow jackets, white ties, and top boots, coachmen in livery, recruiting sergeants, policemen, and every variety of the lesser species of the genus Man, made up the crowd that thronged Ludlow.

The amusements of the day were to consist of — *imprimis* — *déjeuner,* given by Mr. Brassy to a select three hundred or more, at two o'clock in the ballroom. Then, later in the afternoon, rustic sports in the castle green were to delight the riff-raff, and the day was to wind up with a ball which I shall have the pleasure of describing to you directly. In the meantime, I must give a list of the sports in the castle green by the permission of the Right Honorable the Earl of Powis.

PLACARD

*The Rural Sports in the Castle Green by permission of the
Right Honorable the Earl of Powis*

TO COMMENCE AT 2 O'CLOCK

A jingling match by 10 young men — Nine to be blindfolded — Tenth to carry bells — to last one half an hour
— The winner to receive a sovereign — Second best 5s.

JUMPING IN SACKS

Six to start or no race — Each man to find his own sack
— Course the length of the green — Winner to have half a
sovereign — Second best 5s.

NAVVIES TO CLIMB A GREASED POLE FOR A NEW HAT
AND SLOP

SIX BOYS TO EAT TREACLED LOAVES

The successful candidate to receive 5s.

A RACE BY MARRIED WOMEN

Once round the course — Six to start or no race — First
to receive a new metal tea-pot — Second a pound of tea —
Third a pound of coffee.

SINGLE YOUNG WOMEN TO RACE FOR A SOVEREIGN

Ten to start or no race — Twice round the green —
Second best a new gown — Third a pair of stockings.

A RACE OF BOYS 14 YEARS OF AGE

Once round the course. — Winner 5s. — Second best
2s. and 6d. — Twenty to start.

WHEELBARROW RACE

By six navvies — Blindfolded — To find their own bar-
rows — The length of the course — Winner 10s. — Second best 5s.

HURDLE RACE

By young men under 20 years of age — Six to start or no
race — Winner 10s.

TO FINISH WITH

Sweeps dipping for shillings in a tub of flour — Oranges
in water — with their hands tied behind them.

N.B. The Shropshire Yeomanry Band will play on the
Green during the evening for parties who may wish to
dance.

Such was the placard which made its appearance.
The Methodist minister issued his edict against
them in another placard in which he denounced
these sports as degrading and demoralizing, particularly the race on the part of the women. You can
imagine it was no place for us, but Richard went
and was disgusted. Only four married women ran
and no single ones.

Previous to the opening of the gates, there were
shows of various sorts in the street — a clown
dressed up and acting on a very high platform,
ballad-singing, and various things going on. I confess, however, that none of the sports were sufficiently enticing to detain us long in Ludlow, and
we came home to rest and prepare for the ball.

I told you that I should have to get a fresh dress. Accordingly, I commissioned Miss Heightington to send me some samples to choose from, from London. I selected one with four deep flounces, embroidered in silk, and costing, when made, about fifteen dollars, which I found as cheap as anything except tarletan.

But conceive my consternation on Saturday, when I went to try it on, and when Doble, the forewoman, whose name Maria repeats twice and makes a couplet of, "Doble, Doble, toil and trouble" — when, as I before remarked, Doble tried on the corsage, fancy the reflection I made in the glass. The light enters the sanctum of Doble, through yellow shades on either side of the glass, which were certainly not conducive to represent a brilliant complexion. Then, having come in town on horseback, my hair was curled in forez, and flattened to my head by the hat, which at the same time had left on my forehead the usual red mark. Behold me, then, trying on this hopeful dress. Looking in the glass, I saw myself certainly the worse for the light and the hat, but Oh! transcendent compared with the mischief which Doble was designing upon my figure. Drawn tight around the "gorge" and loose around the waist, with the corsage point going almost to the Antipodes was, as you may judge, anything but an encouraging reflection.

However, by dint of letting out in one place and

taking in in another, the dress began to present a better aspect, but it was by no means a *chef d'œuvre*. Then, when it came home yesterday morning, however, it looked altogether much better than I expected. Poor Maria, at the same time, was made the possessor of one of Doble's efforts in white tulle of three skirts trimmed with narrow rows of ribbon.

In addition to minor defects, Maria found it necessary to cut hers down behind, otherwise she was in danger of being choked. I forgot to mention a curious defect in mine, more prominent than in Maria's. This Goble, Doble, Boble, or Toil and Trouble, names given to this barbarian by Maria, facetiously, it might appear, but nevertheless wrung from an agonized spirit — this woman, this ignorant wretch, absolutely gathered the skirt around the long point which I before described, and of course bringing all the fulness in the front. My feelings are better understood than described as I sat altering it. However, Maria made all the fun she could out of our agony and really enjoyed Doble's blunders. They all assured me that the dress was very becoming and looked much better than might have been expected. I have material enough for a new corsage, and the skirt will always be handsome.

Now to the ball. Notwithstanding it has always been the habit of the nobility and gentry of the neighborhood to go to the Charity Balls, which are always mixed, Sir Charles Cuyler took it into his head that this would be much more so and there would be any quantity of drunken navvies, and altogether a horrid set. In consequence, much to the regret of his daughters, he would not go, and perhaps for the same reason, through his influence, the Boughtons were not there; so that the aristocracy included Lord Powis, Willie Kerbery, Mr. Clive, Mr. Robert Clive, another son, ourselves, the Roaches, Miss Beale, the Dunns, Miss Rodney, the Landons, Mr. Betton and Mr. and Mrs. Salway. I danced as before the first dance with Lord Powis, and had no want of engagements for the rest of the evening, even if I had stayed until morning.

The great fun of the evening was in watching the funny costumes and the still more amusing dancing. Nothing could exceed the perfect propriety of the whole affair, nothing boisterous or indecorous in the slightest degree, but Oh! so funny, so funny! Thus ended the great day. We left tolerably early. I am obliged to close as we are going to the Leominster steeple-chase in a few moments.

XVII

MY DEAR H——:

I sent off my letter to you in a great hurry because we were going to the steeple-chase at Leominster. We have been so long without rain, the ground is fearfully hard and so many horses that were entered will not run, and there was such risk of accident that at one time Aunt C. had determined not to go, but we have been and returned!!! My heart still beats with excitement and the scene still dances before my eyes. Let me describe it.

You must know that it is not fashionable for ladies to go, but we, as strangers, can do anything, so that at the appointed hour any number of persons on foot thronged the road between Leominster and the course, but ours was the only carriage. We found that we could not be admitted upon the course in the carriage, but were advised to drive out to an uninhabited cottage where there was a nice veranda which would protect us from the rain that was already beginning to fall. A little path through the garden led us down to a gate within five or six yards of one jump, and commanding a view of several fields and three jumps; and here was such a pretty scene.

On the course were the stand and booths and

people thronging in, and horses in blankets and hoods led up and down by grooms. As a background to this picture rose the large and beautiful church of Leominster, and on either side, in the distance, trees and hills and cottages here and there. The course or line to be run was marked by little yellow flags at certain distances. Seated on the stile, we watched people coming in and speculated upon the merits of the horses that were being walked up and down. As for me, I fell in love with four black legs which was all that I could see for the enormous blanket that hid the rest from my sight. And now the blankets are being removed and the jockeys are going to mount, and my love with the black legs stands revealed, Black Peter, by name, a perfect beauty, notwithstanding Richard says the pastern joint is too long — the distance between fetlock and the hoof.

I am not critical, so that Black Peter is comely in my eyes. And now his jockey mounts, white cap, jacket, and breeches, top boots as brilliant as Peter's own coat. In love, as I am, with Peter, my attention is distracted, for Half-and-Half, ridden by Archer, the best jockey in England, is coming at a canter across the field and is going to take a hedge near us, as a little practice before he begins the race. Richard and I stand breathless. He is at the hedge — he takes it, but he does it clumsily. He redeems himself at the hurdle. Archer wears red cap and jacket and gold bands and white breeches, and with Half-and-Half I am familiar as possible. He was born and trained at Richard's castle. I have seen him out hunting and I have met him exercising on the Vignyles and Hanway; besides, his merits have been one of the most interesting topics of conversation between Henry Landon and myself.

The other horses are Bedford, Little Charlie, and the Unknown. The dresses are so pretty, and what better end could I give to such a sentence than to say that I wish almost that I were a jockey. The exciting moment approaches, crowds hurry to a neighboring hillside which commands a good view, the bell sounds, they are off, but we do not see them yet — they are too far away. Now we catch glimpses of them — they are coming over the hedge. Half-and-Half leads. They are over, and they come across the field towards us at a moderate canter, no faster than Richard and I often ride. We stand within a few yards of them, as they take the hedge. Oh! it is something magnificent, those leaps! We watched them take the hurdle. They gallop on. Half-and-Half leads, and my love is not far behind.

The first round is accomplished. In the second the pace is somewhat accelerated, and Half-and-Half still leads, but now comes the test. We watch with beating hearts as the third round begins, we strain our eyes as they come over the farther hedge, but one is missing. With what anxiety we question

which it is. Alas, Half-and-Half is *hors de combat*.
Now, all my interest is centred in Peter. He leads.
He comes on so light of foot, so light of spirit, but,
to my disgust, a little horse named Charlie begins
to show himself. He is up to Peter. We run down
the course. They have removed the hurdle. At
what a pace they go! The riders call out, they
strain every nerve.

Little Charlie is passing Peter. They near the
winning post, they reach it, and the foremost horse
and man are rolling in the dust. Richard runs to
see what is the matter, but the measure of my
chagrin is full. Peter has lost, and my love, so
black, so beautiful, is vanquished!

Richard soon comes back. Charlie is undeniably
the winner, but, just as he passed the winning post,
he got his foot in a grip and fell. Neither man nor
horse was hurt. As for Half-and-Half, his rider
was shoved up against a tree and his leg severely
injured. I begin to find some consolation in the
assurance that Peter carried such a heavy weight,
ten stone and something over, and Charlie only
eight stone and seven pounds, that he would have
won otherwise.

It is pouring rain while we stand in the course,
and my ardor is so dampened that I am willing to
go into the house. As for Maria, her excitement
has carried her to a most improper extent. To our
consternation, we see her walking at some distance
and approaching the stand with a young man with

whom she has scraped acquaintance. She comes to us after a while and we all go to the house, where Mr. Charlton joins us. There are to be several other races, but Richard is going to Clungunford to stay two days and, as it is fifteen miles distant, we are obliged to hurry home.

Mr. Charlton proposes that each shall put in one shilling and draw the names of certain horses, and whosesoever horse wins shall receive all. Thus it is my lot falls.

April 30th

RICHARD won and my horse came to grief. He got his foot in a grip and fell. We hurried home from the races because Richard is going to Clungunford to dine and pass two days. He returned after enjoying himself exceedingly. The first day all his belles were there, Miss Boughton, Constance Cuyler, and Louisa Roache. They sat down twenty-eight at dinner, had a dance afterward, and most of the dinner-party remained all night, for Clungunford is twelve or fifteen miles from this neighborhood.

Tuesday of last week Richard went to pay a similar visit to Sir William Smith, fifteen miles from this, in Worcestershire. Aunt C. took him in the carriage, so we had an opportunity of seeing quite a new part of the country. On our return, we stopped at Burford to see a little church which has recently been restored. I hardly knew which to admire most, the rectory or the church. The church is chiefly remarkable for its monuments, among which is that of one Richard Cornwall, a knight in full armor lying on his tomb in front of the chancel. He died at the age of twenty and was eight feet tall. The figure, as in many cases here, is in some sort of alabaster.

Another recumbent statue is of a daughter of John of Gaunt, and her dress is copied apparently with great minuteness both in color and even in pattern, upon the material represented. One of Mr. Charlton's ancestors at Ludlow, Sir Job Charlton, is in red robes, and, indeed, in almost all the monuments that I have seen there has been coloring. It gives a peculiarly antique look. This little church at Burford is quite perfect in every respect. It is in the ground belonging, I suppose, to the Rushouts, of whom there are two old maiden sisters and a bachelor brother who take great interest in keeping it in repair.

It would be charming to make a tour through England for the sake of visiting, if nothing else, the parish churches. In this neighborhood, all that I have seen are picturesque and full of interest. I have always fancied that the church and churchyard in Gray's "Elegy" had a beauty peculiar to itself, but it needs only Gray's pen to make as touching and beautiful a picture out of every churchyard.

"These rugged elms, the yew trees shade,
Where heaves the turf in many a mouldering heap."

The quaint habitations, the distant landscape, and the hamlet near by are never wanting.

At Burford, as one walks around the churchyard, one looks through an iron network covering the doorway into the chancel, and there, in the mellowed light from the stained-glass windows and with a stillness rendered doubly solemn by the presence of death, appears in cold relief the mail-clad figure of Richard Cornwall. The effect is very fine and imposing. Within the chancel rails is a curious triptych with doors on which are painted in excellent style pictures of the twelve apostles. It was erected in memory of Richard Cornwall and Janet his wife, and all of the pictures have this motto, "Regard not these pictures, but follow the Lord, as did the apostles in lyff and in word."

Beneath the pictures are verses on scrolls among which are these two:

> "Syth death so certayne is and shuer,
> And so uncertayne is the houer,
> Regard the concell whych I gyve,
> Lyve well to dye, dye well to lyve."

> "For as you are, so once was I,
> And so I am, so shall you be,
> Although that you be fayre and younge,
> Wyse, wealthy, hardy, stout and stronge."

I shall send the "Church Review," with what my mother says she will send me, to Lady Lucy Herbert, who is far more interested in the Church than any of the clergy. I do not know what my mother will say when I tell her more minutely about the clergy. Fancy a clergyman, a Mr. Brown, whom they call "Dodger" Brown, engaging me for a polka at the ball! I did not dance with him, because I did not stay late enough, but I should have had very great scruples about dancing with him if I had known that he was a clergyman.

Thursday, May 6th

WE continue to hear deplorable accounts of the cold weather in America. Since we have had rain, vegetation has advanced rapidly. How much my mother would enjoy the gardens; and fruit trees, so beautifully trained against the walls, are in flower. Indeed, the apricots in the open air are nearly as large as walnuts. We have had strawberries, grown under glass, occasionally and a few at a time since Easter day. As soon as they have got through bearing, those in the open air will be ripening. Asparagus we have had for a long time and radishes.

XVIII

Your last letter came most unexpectedly by the British steamer, but it was not, I assure you, the less acceptable for being unexpected. Now that the time is becoming more definite with regard to our departure, I begin to feel quite impatient. All the pleasure I have enjoyed here, the mode of life so preferable to that in America, and the delightful climate, have not alienated me in the slightest degree from home, though I must confess that, were my mother and you and the children here, I never should care to cross the Atlantic and to leave this old world, so rich in objects of interest, for the new. Apart from the gratification of taste, one can really live in comfort, free from domestic cares, and upon no larger sum than in America would give only half the amount of enjoyment. Then one has so much pleasure in the open air, in the scenery, and in the gardens. I find myself constantly tempted to lay down my pen and look out the window, the scene before me is so lovely. The sun is shining warm and bright and every shade of green decks the landscape.

The colors of the landscape were not to be resisted as they lay before me, and here is what they have effected. I only wish I could put in the cuckoo's note as I hear it every now and then from one of my bedroom windows, than which nothing could be more lovely.

We went last Wednesday to the races at Shrewsbury and enjoyed the day very much. We left Ludlow in the train at quarter past ten and arrived at Shrewsbury at quarter after twelve, thus making the distance of twenty-seven miles in two hours, but when you know that there are ten stations on the way, it is not so very long; still, we were infinitely amused at the free-and-easy way John Bull would pull up and stop for no other purpose apparently than for a quarter of an hour's chat at the different stations — so different from our hurried, go-ahead style. We found on our arrival at Shrewsbury that we had time before lunch and the races for a little sight-seeing. We were so fortunate as to go at once to the Church of St. Mary's, which is the church the best worth seeing in Shrewsbury. It was full of very rich and beautiful stained glass, most of it being very old. It is in a better state of preservation than the church at Ludlow, owing, perhaps, to the very careful restoration made by a wealthy Reverend Mr. Scott of Shrewsbury, a man of some fortune, and a bachelor who spends his substance in restoring the churches about him. I found in the vestry room some exquisite specimens of German painting on glass, dated 1639. In one small window in the various circular compartments was a story of Esther, the others being equally beautiful, but we had time to study out only part of the histories.

The ceiling of the nave was the finest carving that I have seen. We found but few very old monuments, and two modern ones of interest, one the statue seated, and in his robes, of the great Bishop Butler, and the other a tablet with a carving in bas-relief of Admiral Benbow.

Though by no manner of means so large, the effect of St. Mary's is finer than the Ludlow church, for in the former one glance takes in the nave and chancel, the superb eastern window, the partly seen monuments, and the windows of the transept. The organ is at the western end, and if the inside is comparable to the outside, it must be very fine. Within the memory of a person with whom we scraped acquaintance in the train, St. Mary's had as Rector a character in his way — the Reverend Mr. Roland, who scorned the changes of fashion, and continued to eat his dinner at an hour when farmers and ploughmen only dine and gentlemen lunch. Eight o'clock saw the Reverend gentleman comfortably in bed. Indeed, to such an extent did he resist innovations that, when the railway brought among other novelties the Greenwich time, Mr. Roland forbade the alteration of St. Mary's clock, so that during his life many were the travellers who, glancing at St. Mary's clock, said, "Ah, ten minutes more," and found themselves that much too late for the train. If one had much faith in Falstaff, one might naturally expect an imaginary lengthening in time at Shrewsbury, but "the long hour," by the Shrewsbury clock, would be suppressed in these days of steam and science.

We would like to have seen the interior of the abbey, or "h'abbey" as our friend in the train called it, but time closed the doors against us and we saw only the outside, which is very old and very fine. In America one can palliate and excuse liberties and eccentricities in church building, but there appears no excuse for a community placing among these fine specimens of ancient taste a church built in the form of an amphitheatre and dedicated, above all things, to Saint Chad, a Benedictine.

Shrewsbury contains many fine old timbered houses, but none I think equal to the Feathers Inn at Ludlow. We were glad to lunch at the White Lion, though I am almost sorry to lose my association with it, for the hostess, so portly and comfortable in her weeds, did not appear, and, instead of the little room with its bay window and quaint ornaments, we lunched in the plain modern parlor.

I have been remiss in not telling you that "Sans Varier" (Mr. Charlton) accompanied and entertained us, as usual, in his queer, quaint way, which, without its queerness and quaintness of expression, would be prolix, prosy, and profuse. He lunched with us, of course, and went with us to the races. The distance being short between Shrewsbury and the course, we walked, to reach the entrance of which we passed through thimblerig-playing, card-playing, and various other games and pretexts for cheating.

The course was the centre of a motley crowd. There were booths and tents, and boat swings and hand organs, and bands of itinerant musicians, and tumblers for the Punch and Judy exhibits, and bow-and-arrow shooting, and all sorts of people. From the stand, we had a capital view, and, in the intervals between the races, we amused ourselves by watching the people at the betting stands, to which we were so near that we could hear the betting. "I back this horse," "I back that," came to us apparently from every mouth, so that, if I had been ever so much inclined to bet, I should have found it difficult to know whom to take up. It seems to me that the true philosophy is to bet against every horse, and then, as only one can win, you are sure to make enough to make up for that one loss. One never offers to bet in favor here, but against.

We watched with great interest the saddling of the horses and the gray coating of the jockeys. In flat races light weight is very necessary, so that most of these jockeys, if men at all, were men of diminutive size, while many of them were little boys, one of whom looked not more than eight or ten, though they said he was the leader and rode somewhere between four and five stone, about sixty-five pounds. We saw four races, which were quite enough, and we were very happy to find ourselves at the station. We arrived home about half-past eight o'clock, having passed a very pleasant day, the journey over and back costing us five shillings and sixpence, the fare only one way every day.

Thursday, May 20th

UNCLE RICHARD arrived on Sunday, after having posted from Shrewsbury. He had a very pleasant and short passage. He brought the parcel for the contents of which I am very much obliged. With regard to our movements, the present plan seems to be that Aunt C., Richard, Maria, and I shall go to London for a week and then we are to return here, after which we shall arrange for our departure. I see no chance of our being at home before the first of July, for I doubt whether we shall go to London before June.

XIX

My dear H——:

Once more familiar scenes are around me, packed trunks are in the room, and bustle and excitement pervade the house. Aunt C. gives injunctions as they occur to her. She expresses all those anxieties familiar to my mother when she goes down to New York for a night. Indeed, the note of preparation has been sounded and to-morrow at eight o'clock we are off for London. Richard does not go with us, but waits until his father's return in a week or less to the Moor, then he comes up to London.

One topic and one prospect engross us — Aunt C. and Maria are to be presented at Court on Thursday, the 3rd. From the moment we get to London until after the Coronation, as Uncle Richard calls it, nothing will be thought of or seen but dressmakers and milliners. Three mantua-makers are already engaged, so that everything is *en train*. I, of course, have never for a moment entertained the thought of being presented. Aunt C. will ask for a ticket for me to stand on the staircase at the palace with a maid probably, and see the Queen and everybody go up, which will be almost as fine as a spectacle. There will be a state ball at the palace on the 16th, to which Aunt C. and Maria will, no doubt, have tickets, only those, of course, being invited who have been presented. Richard, like myself, will not have the advantage of going to the British Court, as gentlemen are not presented when ladies are at a drawing-room, but at a levée, and I believe there is not more than one of the latter in a season.

We have invitations for dinner at Mrs. Russell Sturgis's to meet a party of Americans on Wednesday at half-past seven. Lady Harriet has been most kind in writing frequently, sending the addresses of her work-people and expressing great interest and kindness, and I am quite sure that we shall be treated with attention by them all. With these prospects my wardrobe presents rather a forlorn aspect. The dress that Miss Heightington made will require altering and remodelling, and I must get a dinner dress. Indeed, Aunt C. thinks everything cheaper than in Paris. It is a great mistake to suppose fashionable English women dowdy and negligent in their dress. The Clives and Powises dress very elegantly.

The prospect of coming home is receding and receding. Aunt C. cannot bear the idea of our leaving, and now we have to come back here from London, and she tells everybody that we shall not leave for some time. The other day Mr. Longworth invited us to go over to Bromfield Rectory to a late lunch, or an early dinner as you please, and to walk through the gardens at Oakly Park, and see the hawthorn in full bloom.

The Cuylers are to be invited to meet us and Mr. and Mrs. Phillips from London and a young Aldersey, lately come from London, because he cannot live in London and keep hunters and drive tandem. He does not get on with his governor. Chester, he says, cannot hold two Alderseys. He is very rapid and looks very young; his clothes are perfectly new and fresh cut in a fast style. He talks loud and calls people familiarly by their surnames, thinks he is funny and tries to make others of the same opinion, talks in an offhand style of his travels in Spain and Italy, and quotes his governor's house and stables and gardens, and is altogether innocent and fatiguing. This is the impression I received of him as he stood in a bay window talking to the little Count de Croymier, who, by the way, does not condescend to talk much to women. If you could only hear that high, imperious little voice, half French and half English, and see the fierce little moustache, upturned to you on a line with your belt, you would be amused. Enough of the Count — "Though he be little, he is fierce." If I give up any more space to him, my London sheets will be crowded.

Looking around the circle, then, to which there were additions we did not expect, just as I was walking along, first with one and then another, a soft voice behind addressed me and a person that I

had observed without knowing who he was joined
me. I looked at him, as I had an indistinct feeling
that I had seen him before. His voice and manner
were very prepossessing and, little by little, the
truth broke upon me until I at last discovered that
this was no other than the Reverend Mr. Wilson,
Rector of Church Stretton, considered very handsome, very vain, and a great lady-killer. Everything was very pleasant but the lunch. Mr. Longworth's bachelor establishment was not elastic
enough for so large a party, and, as Mr. Aldersey
and I came in last, there was only room enough
at the table for me. Mr. Aldersey, after trying
to squeeze himself into impossible places, finally
seated himself at the side table, from which he
would every now and then pop up exclaiming, "I
say, Longworth, the lady wants something more."

The long twilight or rather daylight until half-
past nine o'clock made the evening pleasant, and
we got home at half-past ten, rather tired as one
always is after such long days. I do not know why
it is that a lunch is so much more tiring than a
dinner and dance.

June 1st, '52, London

THE journey yesterday from eight o'clock until
four brought us to this great metropolis. I sit writing to you in our drawing-room at Patterson's
Hotel. I can hardly realize that I am in London or
what is before me. The sun streams in brightly

through the open window, far off we hear the distant roll of carriages, otherwise we are almost as quiet as at the Moor. We arrived yesterday just as the fashionable world were rolling in splendid equipages to Hyde Park, and nothing as a first impression could have given us a more imposing idea of London's greatness; beautiful carriages, yellow generally, with crests and coronets emblazoned on the panels and put on every imaginable part of the harness, and drawn by superb horses, perfectly groomed, and footmen with long stick hanging on behind; fat, red-faced coachmen seated on the box, holding the reins with an indescribable air; fine aristocratic women within, and hundreds of such equipages thronged the streets. But what interested me most were the hansom cabs, odd-looking things tipped back in a comical way, not unlike a chaise, drawn by one horse and a driver seated behind, holding his reins above the roof. These drive like mad through the crowded thoroughfares, poking their horses' noses into all sorts of impossible places. Unfortunately, women never drive in them, otherwise I should like immensely to try one.

As soon as we wiped off our travellers' dust, we set off for Madame Fusey's, the Court dressmaker. After much deliberation, it was decided that Aunt C.'s dress should be corsage and train of pink taffeta and petticoat of white silk or satin, trimmed *en tablier* with Brussels lace, the train to be trimmed with ruching, tulle, and roses. Maria's will be blue glacé, train and corsage and white petticoat trimmed with white lilacs, etc. This morning, we go to the coiffeur.

Mrs. Lawrence sent in the names on cards, several days before, because the Queen requires to know the names of all those to be presented. Everything is *en train*. On our return from Madame Fusey's we found cards from the Russell Sturgises to remind us of the dinner on Wednesday. Uncle R. met Mr. Peabody in the street and, after dinner, Aunt C. and Uncle R. and Maria went to spend the evening with him. I was too tired and lay down on the sofa and went to sleep.

This morning business began. Before breakfast a note was received from Lady Harriet Clive, regretting their absence in the country, and saying they should be back on Thursday, and she would call at five o'clock to know how the Drawing-Room was got through, giving much valuable advice and regretting over and over again her absence. They have made a party for us to go to Eton on Friday, to see the grand fête of the School, boat-racing and fireworks. They will entertain us there; besides, we believe we are to go to Windsor and won't be back until eight at night.

· We are in Brook Street, very near Lady Harriet, who lives in Grosvenor Street. At this moment Madame Fusey is upstairs fitting Aunt C. and Maria. As soon as she gets through, we are going out shopping. All is hurry, and we must have fresh costumes for the Friday party. In London anything can be done, but particularly as we have three dressmakers engaged.

This is a small family hotel. Our parlor is very nice, and so is Aunt Catherine's room, but as yet Maria and I are compressed into a very small space; however, we change to-morrow. Everything is in the usual London style; a butler and three footmen serve our dinner. Shaw is with us and Uncle R. has engaged a carriage for all the time we are here. Fischer was left at home with the children, but a maid is engaged to supply her place, so we are well provided for.

Wednesday, June 2nd

I STOPPED writing yesterday to get ready to go out. We went to Mrs. Lawrence's immediately. I did not go in because I was too shabby, but I sat in the carriage while Shaw pointed out to me everything of interest. The Lawrences live in a fine large house in Piccadilly belonging to Lord Dungannon. On one side lives the Duchess of Gloucester, and on the other the Earl of Rosemeath, I think. Apsley House, the Duke of Wellington's, is very grand and immense, and is not far off. Facing me was the statue of the noble Duke, just at the entrance to Hyde Park, and looking exactly as represented.

Shaw's delight was unbounded in pointing out all these great things. His austere countenance never relaxes into a smile, but when he mentions a great name, then the expansiveness of his smile is marvellous. Fancy, then, the gratification he felt when he told me that the Duchess of Gloucester was coming. She is aunt to the Queen and a daughter-in-law of George the Third, and consequently her turn-out was very fine. Two outriders, four horses, and two postillions and two footmen completed the plain and elegant equipage of this fat, English-looking dowager. I saw, too, the best four-in-hand in England — Sir Harry Peyton, driving his drag.

Aunt C. found Mrs. Lawrence as dowdy and shabby as ever, but very kind. We were shopping before dinner, and between five and seven we went to Hyde Park, where we saw the most magnificent display of equipages, but Rotten Row was the galaxy of my delight — such horses, such horsewomen — ah, dear me! most fortunately we saw the Queen. Shaw warned us of her approach, and in another moment two outriders in red appeared, which was the signal for the carriages to form in line on each side, and she passed between them in an open barouche drawn by four horses, two postillions, of course, two footmen in the rumble and two outriders behind. The Queen wore a pink bonnet, and her face and nose particularly were very red. Prince Albert looked very handsome. The Prince of Wales is a nice-looking boy; the Princess Royal I could not catch a glimpse of. One poor American head ought not to take in more in one day than the Queen and the Crystal Palace, the latter of which is much larger and grander than I had imagined.

London strikes one as very magnificent. As yet I have seen only residences and shops, but they are very grand. The parks are beautiful, there is such perfect order and cleanliness; there is no crowding in the streets, no poor. The wonder is where all the splendid carriages come from, for one cannot go into a street which is not full of them. The truth is that I can give you a very imperfect impression of what I see, for I write against time. I ought to be getting ready for Mrs. Lawrence's now.

Mrs. Bates called this morning and said that twenty-five Americans were to dine to-day with Mrs. Sturgis. I hear of being in town Mrs. George Baty Blake, Mrs. Lispenard Stewart, and Mrs. John Murray, and others that I do not know. I shall not see Aunt C. and Maria dress to-morrow, for tickets are lying on the table now for the meeting of all the charity children in London, which is something very grand, and Uncle R. and I are going at ten o'clock. You can find in Mrs. Coleman's letters an account of it. Maria goes to the opera on Friday night, and perhaps we do, through the kindness of Mr. George Peabody, who sends us tickets. I shall certainly go on Saturday night through his politeness. This is the plan for this week.

Thursday, June 3rd

To-DAY has produced two such interesting events
that I do not know where to begin. In order to see
the children at St. Paul's, I had to give up seeing
the people going to the Drawing-Room, and we
left this house even before they were dressed. I
only saw Maria's head finished, and I have this
moment returned from St. Paul's, but Aunt C. and
Maria have not yet arrived. I have witnessed at
once the most touching and the most sublime sight
I ever expect to see, the Drawing-Room to the contrary, notwithstanding. To reach St. Paul's we
drove through classic ground, passing through the
Strand and Fleet Street and through the Temple
Bar, saw the lane leading to the various courts of
law, and finally drew up before St. Paul's, which,
to be sure, is very grand, very large, and exactly
like the pictures of it, with the addition of a good
deal of smoke and soot. Our tickets permitted the
carriage to come up to the gate, where we got out,
and, walking through the yard, entered the north
entrance.

The interior of St. Paul's is like a cross, thus,
— ⊕ — the dome being the circle. Entering, then,
this grand edifice, we found most of the ground
floor filled with spectators, while rising from the
floor and running around the dome and back to the
top of the cross, up against the organ, were benches,
fifteen tiers high. They were to accommodate the
children, ten thousand of them. Uncle R. calcu-

lates five thousand, for the largest opera house in the world will hold only forty-five hundred persons.

We arrived at eleven o'clock, and the services were not begun until twelve, so that but few of the schools had entered, which gave us time to watch them carefully. One school at a time entered and was placed, rails running down and separating them. Now girls came in, one school in brown, another in red, another in blue, another in green, in gray, and so on through all the colors, but they all wore caps, picturesque and lovely, but of various patterns, some with very high crowns, some with low, but all either plain or quilted borders, setting off such healthy, happy faces as rejoiced one to see. They all wore little white handkerchiefs or capes, and white aprons. Many schools had medals hung around the necks by a bright ribbon. Some wore rosettes, and one school had each a white rose at the waist.

The boys looked very nicely, some schools in coats and some in jackets, but all being provided with either rosettes or bouquets. Thus they came in and were arranged with such order and quietness — now the boys above, and the girls below, now girls filing up to the top, until finally the circle was complete. In the upper part of the cross was, I told you, the choir and organ, and rising immediately above the children were the white-robed choristers, at least one hundred in number. This, as you can imagine, was a magnificent *coup d'œil*, but, when the clergyman entered the desk, on a level with the organ and almost out of sight, and the whole assemblage of children rose, and the little girls lifted their aprons to their faces, like angels folding their wings in prayer, and the boys placed each a hand over his eyes, it was touching beyond description. The service began by the whole assemblage, choir and children and spectators singing the "Old Hundred," which was very grand, though to my ear "Old Hundred" always sounds flat sung by a number of persons. After the hymn, I heard a sonorous voice, ringing clear through that great church, like a ringing bell, intoning the service.

In the Dearly Beloved the clergyman read one sentence and the choir in the same tone chanted the next, but in the Confession, they joined in chanting it in one sustained note, until the Amen, when the high clear voices of these little ones swelled the note as it changed to one higher and rolled through the arches and died away in the dome. Then again in the Lord's Prayer the same sublime effect was produced. In the sentences following the Lord's Prayer, the clear voice of the priest scarcely died in the distance, when the note was taken up by the choir and children and then one heard again the sound as of a speaking bell. The Venite Psalms for the day were chanted to one of our familiar double chants by all. The lessons were intoned, and, though I was so far off, I could follow in the second lesson. The Te Deum and

Jubilate were sung by the choir and were magnificent. Before the prayer for the Queen (it was not a litany day) the Coronation Anthem was sung, the children joining in the chorus; then there was a psalm before the sermon by our Bishop of Hereford, and after the sermon again another psalm, and finally the Hallelujah Chorus.

How can I describe to you the effect of the Coronation and the Hallelujah Chorus! — these children singing in such perfect time, in such perfect tune, and so entirely in unison that it sounds like one voice. There was something wonderful in the organ, in the Gloria Patri, and the sesquialtera stood out so boldly and piercingly that I thought, at first, that some instrument must have been used, perhaps to keep up the pitch. The effect was superb, as its sharp, cutting notes reverberated through the church. The sub-bass was very powerful and produced a great effect; indeed, the whole was something that can be heard only in England, and once heard can never be forgotten. The latter part of the service was rendered very painful by many of the children fainting.

Aunt C. and Maria returned from the Drawing-Room at four o'clock, earlier than usual, because, being the last one of the season, not more than eighty were presented. They got through very successfully and found it by no means so formidable as they expected. I must tell you now about the dresses. The colors you know; the effect is what you want. On one side of the head are three or four ostrich feathers which are curled under and hang low on it. There are flowers, and from behind hangs a blonde barb called lappets. The corsage is as usual. The train of the same is put around the waist almost to the point. It may be trimmed with lace and made, of course, superb. Aunt C.'s was trimmed with tulle and roses and Maria's with tulle and lilacs. The petticoat may be trimmed *en tablier* or with flounces. It is a most becoming dress, and both Maria and Aunt C. looked uncommonly well, Maria better than I ever saw her.

They went to Mrs. Lawrence's at one, had cards to admit their carriage through the embassadors' gate, then, besides, both Maria and Aunt C. had a card with her name written on it thus, "Mrs. Fay" or "Miss Fay, of the United States, presented by Mrs. Lawrence." One card was left on the green board at the entrance. The other was given to some gentleman official in the throne room, who passed it in to another, going through several hands, until it reached the Queen, who read the name out in a loud tone of voice. They entered the throne room with the general circle, that is, after the diplomats and people belonging to the Government. Maria said that she thought of Bunker Hill and went on. Before entering the throne room their trains were spread out by pages. They curtsied twice to the Queen, once after their names were announced and the other time after the Queen had bowed. They curtsied also to Prince Albert and to the Royal family, and then pages took up their trains and placed them over their arms and they were at the door. The great event was over. They sat after this in the embassadors' corner of the room, where only diplomats or persons presented by them, and privileged people, remained, saw the others presented, while Mrs. Lawrence pointed out all the great people.

The most magnificent dresses and diamonds were worn by Miss Burdett-Coutts, the Countess Brunow, the Russian Embassadress, and the Duchess of Northumberland. They were there very much entertained by the Indian Princes and saw a great deal to interest them.

St. James's Palace was shabby. I shall see almost as much, so you need not regret my not being presented, for Lady Harriet is to get us an invitation to the Duchess of Northumberland's Saturday week. Then Lady Harriet is to have a ball on the thirteenth, and I shall have plenty of opportunities of seeing the great people.

Friday

WE are going to Eton this morning. Good-by; love to all.

XX

My dear Mother:

I am so much ashamed of the letter that I sent you from London, that I seize the first disengaged moment that the quiet and tranquillity of the Moor has given me, to endeavor to redeem myself. You can imagine what with sight-seeing all the morning and being out all night until broad daylight, I should not have had much time to write you, to convey to you an impression of all that gave me pleasure. I find myself, when I do attempt to write, far too tired to give anything more than a very matter-of-fact description. Aunt C. was so unwell all the time we were in London that she seldom went anywhere with us, and, when we were at home, she liked me either to talk to her or to read to her.

We arrived home last evening about nine o'clock after a series of adventures that needed only an upset to have made the journey from Oxford to the Moor a chapter of accidents; travelling from Oxford to Gloucester on the Great Western Railway at intervals at the rate of sixty miles an hour, accidents happening to other trains delayed us half an hour, so that, when we arrived at Gloucester, the train that we should have taken to Worcester had gone, leaving us to decide between coach or post to complete more than sixty miles of our journey. Coach has the advantage of being able to carry any amount of luggage of which, though we tried to reduce our necessities, we have three trunks and a hat-box.

Mr. Landon of the party adds his mite in portmanteau and carpetbag. Our seats then are taken. I make one of four inside, Maria, Mr. Landon, and Richard, three of seven outside. Thus we journey from Gloucester to Ross, my inside fellow-travellers being an invalid lady, a pretty country girl, and an elderly gentleman, a Mr. Arkwright, whose father was a great cotton spinner and left him a fine fortune and a beautiful country place somewhere between Hereford and Leominster. I do not enjoy much the society of my fellow-travellers. The invalid lady speaks in so low a tone that I have to beg her pardon and regret I did not hear. The elderly gentleman is deaf, begs my pardon, is sorry he has his bad ear towards me, and even when my most distinct tones are employed I find he looks embarrassed and answers distractedly. The country girl says nothing.

At Ross, Maria and I exchange seats. I find myself perched up behind, for the top of the coach is used for luggage. The country is lovely between Ross and Hereford, and I am glad once more to see hill and dale. Even the softness and beauty of the English landscape always does not compensate for the sameness we found from Shrewsbury to London, and from London again to Gloucester. So charming is the country after this that at Hereford we take all outside seats. One sees here the effect of no railway. We are so long in getting off that the coachman at last falls into a passion because a poor woman is hopelessly trying to find a seat and is rejected on all sides. "I should think," says the coachman, "that you people in the country were all asleep; I wonder what you will do when the train comes." At last we are off, when suddenly the old woman, who has been perched up near us, finds that her old man is left behind. The first thing that I know her umbrella goes flying over my head from her outspread hands. She calls to the coachman to stop, and I prepare for her taking the same eccentric course her umbrella did. A man jumps off and prevents her throwing herself off, but she is not to be foiled. She gets down; she calls for her basket, and is away to her old man. We fancy ourselves now comfortably under way, when suddenly a spring threatens to break. The guard, poor man, has no seat, the coach is so crowded, and hanging on to the spring, it is not surprising that it should break. However, they tell us it will last, and so again we compose ourselves; but the comfort is short-lived. It begins to rain; we are enveloped in blankets and shawls and umbrellas are raised, and the rain, instead of falling upon us in drops, rains down upon us in streams from the points of the umbrellas. As we near Leominster the rain ceases and bright sky appears just as we are comfortably in the fly which soon lands us safely at the Moor.

We enjoyed the visit to Oxford. Our visit was like that of the angels to poor Mr. Rich, who had not spoken to a young lady since he left Cambridge. He treasures every remembrance of his life there, and he still has the flower he took from H. He showed us through many of the colleges and we saw the great library. When one has seen one college, one has seen all, with a few exceptions. They all have cloisters. The interior of New Chapel and Magdalene Chapel are very fine; indeed, in New Chapel the interior is wonderful. Another curious thing is that the choir organ is in a stone case. I had been prepared to see in Oxford some of Sir Christopher Wren's beautiful pictures, but I confess I had not been prepared for the vandalism of painting the beautiful oak ceiling a lead color. In one case there was a painted canopy drawn over the oak roof. Now New College, although it bear the name of New, is five hundred years old, and the chapel has been most beautifully restored. Maria and Mr. Rich went to chapel in the afternoon, but Richard and I went out in a boat, Richard taking the part of oarsman and I coxswain. I proved quite a wonder at steering and brought our little boat into the wharf in the most admirable manner.

As there are nineteen colleges and several halls

at Oxford, it would have been rather severe to go through all of them, when I tell you that I did not go to bed until four o'clock the night before and got up at half-past seven to start in the train.

Our dinner at Blackwall turned out very pleasantly, though we had previously imagined it a great bore. Young Russell, of Boston, who had just arrived from America, went with us. Fancy seeing one hundred of our compatriots that one had never seen before; in all directions the tones that reached us were undeniably American. Among the party assembled were the Lawrences, two Miss Morrisons from Carolina, who have been belles in New York, Mrs. Stewart and Miss Rhinelander, and the rest I did not know, except, indeed, the Griswolds, and Bigot and Abbelow Lawrence (a mistake Mrs. Lawrence once made in introducing her two sons), who arrived about the same time, who were to take us down to dinner, and through Richard's intervention I fell to Mr. Russell.

The dining-room was a great big room, as you can imagine to dine one hundred and twelve persons. There I found myself seated at a branch of the great table. Sometimes I found Mr. Russell quite pleasant enough, and it was not for some time that the light attentions of my other neighbor caused me to turn. As soon as he obtained my attention, he began to talk to me, and then I found him to be a churchman and a clergyman, the Reverend Mr. Weston, one of the rectors of Trinity, New York, full of zeal, and he made himself very agreeable. He is the strongest sort of churchman, with great pride in and admiration for Harry of Exeter, and regretted the loss of the Athanasian Creed in our liturgy. I do not know when we should have stopped talking if Mr. Russell had not manifested some impatience.

The whitebait, for which every one goes to Blackwall, are about the size or a little larger than shrimp. They are white and soft, and one eats them with lemon and cayenne. The dinner was most sumptuously supplied with wines and dessert, strawberries and grapes in profusion, which must have been raised under glass, and are immensely expensive. Mr. Peabody does everything on the most liberal scale. The two nights that he sent us tickets for the opera, he had two or three boxes full, and every lady he supplied with a choice bouquet. He is an excellent man, but not the most elegant. Though Englishmen, as a general thing, are not as agreeable by far as Americans, yet there is an elegance in their manner of speaking, a degree of high breeding which I have missed in those Americans with whom I have compared them since I have been here. I was very much disappointed in the dancing beaux I saw at Lady Harriet's and Lady Powis's. They were not particularly *distingué* and very young-looking, quite the boyish set one sees at home. At the Caledonian Ball were any quantity of handsome guardsmen and military men, and they were magnificent — but to return to the dinner.

After the dessert the toasts began with one to the Queen, followed by another to the President of the United States. Mr. Peabody's health was then drunk and the American Minister's, which brought Mr. Lawrence out in a speech which did very well until at the end he apologized for not entertaining his American friends as Mr. Peabody did, which certainly was in bad taste, a thing no foreign minister does. It was very coldly received, as you may imagine. When Mr. Lawrence got through, we very quickly withdrew, for being eleven o'clock it was time we should begin to get ready for Lady Powis's, particularly as we had five miles to drive. We wore high silk dresses at the dinner. As it was, we did not get to Lady Powis's until about twelve o'clock; however, we avoided the long file, which is so tiresome.

Lord Powis's house is not larger than most of the New York houses. The dancing was upstairs in two rooms without carpeting, and there was yet a third room, quite small, but always comfortably empty. The dancing-rooms were the most perfect crush that can be imagined. I danced once with Richard, and John Roache asked me for another, but I declined because I did not know how well he danced. I preferred to sit by Lady Harriet Clive and talk with her. Lady Harriet, though she is a little stately at first, is the most amiable, charming, kind, and considerate person that ever lived, and then she is thoroughly good and noble; there is no end to the good she does. She is always exceedingly kind in expressing her approval and admiration of my dress.

I had again the pleasure of seeing the beautiful Ladies St. Maur. Lady Clementine Villers has long been considered a great belle. Mary Clive says Lord Powis likes her very much. She is certainly a very fine, aristocratic-looking woman. I have seen almost all the nobilities; only think how unfortunate, that at Northumberland House I was in the same room with the Duke of Wellington, but did not see him; indeed, I did not see anything of him except his equestrian statue over the entrance to Hyde Park, which is quite as absurd as "Punch" has represented him.

The Duchess of Northumberland was at Lady Powis's and invited us again for Saturday. We saw the celebrated and eccentric Lord Ward, and Lady Ward, his mother, invited Aunt C. to pay her a visit at Henley. Another person to whom we were presented, whom you will be interested in, was Miss Burdett-Coutts. She is a tall, thin woman, about forty, whose face, notwithstanding a painful eruption which covers it, wears an expression of great sweetness and goodness, and she is well liked. She does a vast deal of good. She has endowed two bishoprics and built two churches in London. Doctor Wainwright told her that her name was a household word among churchmen of America.

Aunt C. and Maria were invited to dine one evening at Mrs. Lawrence's, and Richard and I came afterwards. Miss Coutts and the Duke of Rutland were of the party, but the Duke had left when we arrived. Mrs. Lawrence in some respects lives in fine style, but there are many inconsistencies in it. Miss Clive says that Mr. Lawrence is very much liked, he is so very ready and has always something pleasant to say, but Mrs. Lawrence has her peculiarities; however, they say her very independence is liked.

I suppose I have got to be very critical, but I really felt quite hurt because, when Richard and I came, our names were not cried out at the foot of the stairs, taken up by the footman at the top, and transferred to the groom of the chambers. I felt quite like resenting our being asked our names at the drawing-room door. We had been previously invited to the Marchioness of Westminster's, but Mrs. Lawrence, who calls herself her particular friend, informed her that she was going to bring us.

As I told you, we were an hour in file, which brought it to twelve o'clock, after which we were to go to Lady Harriet's. The Marquis of Westminster is the richest peer in England, and the Grosvenor Gallery is very celebrated. The house is very large and filled with the most perfect works of art and fine-looking men and women, and one

could see no finer *coup d'œil.* Lady Westminster
was so kind as to tell us that she would give orders
to have us admitted whenever we might call,
though the regular day for opening the house to the
public who are so fortunate as to obtain tickets is
Thursday. Thus we were happy to see this great
house by daylight.

I think I remember quite perfectly most of the
great pictures. In one room there are four magnificent Rubens. This collection contains Reynolds's great picture of Mrs. Siddons as the Tragic
Muse; I saw Reynolds's other portrait of her at the
Vernon Gallery; Titian's Mistress, and several
other pictures of his; such Claudes as I never hoped
to see; Murillo's St. John and the Lamb; a wonderful landscape by Berghen, several Julio Romanos,
Wouvermans, Rembrandts, Carlo Dolce, Sasso
Ferrato, Canaletto, Raphael, Salvator Rosa, Paul
Potter, Permegiano, Gainsborough, Collins, and
many other celebrated artists were the men whose
pictures we saw. Then there were some fine statu-
ary and many objects of the greatest *vertu;* a
malachite vase, for example, which cost some eight
thousand pounds, and two tables with slabs of
lapis-lazuli, small to be sure, but very rare and
costly.

In my last letter I think I told you that we would
not go to Lady Harriet's much before one o'clock,
and we needed no candle to go to bed by. I know
you will rejoice that I have had an opportunity of

seeing so much more, perhaps more than many American young ladies have, of such distinguished society, and the pleasure and the benefit which I trust I have derived have not been so much because they are titled and rich people, but because it is elevating and improving to associate with people so thoroughly well-bred, so cultivated, and so amiable and hospitable.

We went with Lady Harriet to the Chiswick flower show. There was no end of the kindnesses of the Clives. Richard rode twice in Rotten Row with Robert Clive, and we saw them very often. We enjoyed nothing more than the galleries of water-color paintings. You can have no idea of the exquisite perfection to which water-colors have been brought in England. At the Vernon Gallery we saw many of the old French masters, together with Reynolds, Sir Thomas Lawrence, and others. One day we passed at Hampton Court, examining the many pictures there, all the beauties of the Court of Charles the Second.

While we were waiting at the inn for the rain to hold up, some gypsies offered to tell our fortunes, and you can imagine we jumped at the chance. Two lovers were described for me; the first was not very carefully pictured, but the second was said to be tall and handsome and between dark and light. For Maria a supposed journey was foretold; and for Richard a kiss from the lady of his love.

I wrote you that we were going to Westminster

to service for the first time, and we went in the afternoon to the Temple Church, built by the ancient Templars. Our visits to the British Museum and the Bank of England were the only things of which I have not written you, but then, if I don't keep something back, I shall have nothing to tell to make myself agreeable when I return. We had two drawbacks to our pleasure in Aunt Catherine's illness and in the weather. We should have enjoyed everything so much more if Aunt C. had been able to go with us, instead of leaving her at home and suffering. Lady Harriet sent her her doctor, who has benefited her a great deal, so that now she is quite like herself.

The rainy weather was anything but pleasant, but still we were not prevented from going out. Week after next we are invited to go to make Mrs. Stackhouse-Acton a little visit, when she will take us on a sketching excursion. She has a fine old place at Church Stretton, and we shall enjoy it very much.

XXI

My dear H——:

It is now nearly three weeks, or quite I should say, since I heard from home, and I should be exceedingly anxious but that I fancy you think me on my way home. But here I am still and cannot even tell you when we shall leave. Aunt C. will not hear of Maria and I coming out without the protection of some one, and the rub is to find such a person as we should like. Uncle Richard has written Mr. Lowell, who goes out soon, and I trust before this letter goes to know his answer.

By this time you must know all about our visit to London, and I am quite sure you have rejoiced in all the opportunities I have had of seeing the *beau monde.* I trust, my dear H., your day is to come; for myself, I believe I am improved by all the advantages I have had; at least, I have tried to appropriate all I have seen and heard that I might share with you and my mother some of the pleasure which has cost so long an absence.

I doubt whether I told you how much I liked the opera. I heard all the great singers except Grisi — Mario, Lablache, Julienne Castelan, Cruvelli, and Ronconi, and, strange as it may seem, I was not so wonderfully impressed as I expected. Both the houses are so immensely large that one does not appreciate the power of the voices. Mario and Lablache make no greater effect than Benedetti did in his palmy days at the little opera-house in Astor Place. I found myself much more impressed by the exquisite scenic effects, the great number of the operatic corps, and the whole beautiful spectacle, than by the beauty of the voices. True, I only heard Mario in the Zauberflöte, in which there is but little opportunity for a display of his power. At Covent Garden we saw Robert le Diable in Zauberflöte and at Her Majesty's Il Barbiere. In the latter Lablache is capital. Nothing can be more comic than the Falstaffian figure skipping about the stage. He appears all the more comic because the part of Il Barbiere was performed by Beletti, who went out with Jenny Lind, and who was a miserable stick of an actor. At this theatre they say the ballet is quite as good as in Paris. Certainly to me it was exquisite.

I confess the three nights at the opera in London was a bad preparation for the theatricals with which Mr. Ponsferd enlivens the otherwise dull summer months in Ludlow.

"Rustic, sir, quite rustic," said he to Richard, as with a wave of the hand he received Richard's application for the best seat on a late occasion when Robert Clive was the patron of the night. And rustic we found it, and exceedingly entertaining. There were three plays announced — "The

Used-up Man," "Uncle Jerry," and "A Screaming Farce." Fancy a square room divided into pit, dress-circle, and gallery, lined with striped paper, the walls hung with matting made of rushes, and the whole lighted with gas-burners without shades. The stage was brought so close that there remains now to me not the vestige of a delusion with regard to the arts practised upon us. This close proximity of the *dramatis personæ* and the audience gave the former the advantage of keeping the latter in order. In the midst of a grand solo part, in which Sir Charles Coldstream (Mr. Ponsferd), *ennuyant* of the world and retired into the character of a ploughman, gives the audience his confidence in that open manner peculiar to the stage — in the midst of this confidential monologue, Mr. Ponsferd stopped and addressed some one in the gallery.

"You, sir, if you cannot stop talking, please depart, and you will find your money at the door; otherwise I shall call the police."

"I am not the person you allude to," replied the man.

Mr. Ponsferd persisted in believing him to be the culprit, but as silence ensued there was no need of further parley.

But let me hasten to do tardy justice to the orchestra. We came in at an *entr'acte*, and nothing can exceed the measured malice of the music that saluted our ears, produced by three violins and a violoncello. The performer upon the latter made two notes serve as bass, what Charles Lamb would call a "thorough bass," for it was supereminently harsh and disagreeable.

The violinists, disdainful alike of a vulgar prejudice in favor of harmony, followed each one his own fancy rather than that of the composer. To their credit be it said, a Ludlow audience could not sit by patiently and see its favorite waltzes murdered without interfering. If hisses could do any good, harmony would have resumed its sway.

Theodore Beale was with us and accompanied us to the theatre, and we sat in Robert Clive's box, which, on the night when Lady Harriet patronizes the play, is ornamented with flowers and white cambric. The Ludlow races came off the 30th of June and 1st of July. I only went the first day. The course is one of the prettiest in England, a smooth green plain within an amphitheatre of hills. Some of the races were very good, but the second, which is the more fashionable day of the two, they were very poor. I did not go and thereby missed seeing Constance Cuyler, between whom and myself quite an intimacy has sprung up, so that we correspond.

Since the first of July we have had summer weather. The sun shines in a cloudless sky, but it does not parch and scorch. Under its genial warmth the grass looks greener and the trees darker and richer. The air is fragrant with honeysuckle and roses, and the strawberries are riper and of a finer flavor. We dine at seven o'clock, and after dinner we stroll about the garden, sometimes through the dingles, until nine and after. Indeed, at ten o'clock it is hardly dark. It is delightful, these long summer evenings, the sky overhead so delicately blue, softened off in the west into such a lovely shade of pink, not glaring like our sunsets. Through this heat has come the dissolution of Parliament, and the elections for a new Parliament. The borough of Ludlow sends two men, who have been Mr. Henry Clive, cousin of our friends, and Colonel Salway, a violent Radical. Mr. Clive of Oakly Park was formerly member for Ludlow, but not long ago it turned him out and the County returned him. Now Mr. Henry Clive retires and makes way for young Robert Clive, who is sure to be returned. The contest lies between Lord William Powlett, brother of the Duke of Cleveland, and Colonel Salway. Robert Clive has been down at Oakly Park for more than a week, canvassing. It is necessary that a candidate should go and see every elector and solicit his vote, and when one considers that he has to play the agreeable to all sorts of people, it is not so pleasant; as, for example, Robert Clive had to go to Major Stevenson's to solicit his servants' votes. It is somewhat odd that the women hold such sway here and have such influence upon votes that they have to be sedulously courted.

To-day, Wednesday, July 7th, we went to see

the nomination at Guild Hall in Ludlow, and as we drove through the town we saw the colors of each candidate conspicuous in banners and cockades. A band attached to each party produced at various corners of the streets anything but harmonious sounds. We were so fortunate as to get into the reserved seats for ladies, though we came late; but after all there is not much choice of a comfortable situation on a warm day when one has a narrow wooden seat, although it be a sort of pew, for we were surrounded by a heated, promiscuous, and not very delicately scented crowd, but my strong nerves can bear wonders. Soon after we got in, the doors were opened and the crowd rushed in. Then began the proceedings.

The clerk, in a nasal voice, and with a very imperfect perception of what he had to read, cried, "Oyez, Oyez," etc., when the Mayor read several acts of Parliament on bribery, which were as clear and concise as most worshipful legislators take a pleasure in making their laws. Nevertheless the clerk cried at the end of each, "God save the Queen," so I suppose they must have been quite just and right. The candidates and their supporters (two for each) were seated on a platform divided, the Radicals from the Conservatives, by His Worship the Mayor. Each candidate had for his supporters a gentleman and a burgher, both of whom successively presented the persons for whom he solicited the votes of the electors. I was glad to have this opportunity of hearing the principles of each party declared. Colonel Salway is a true Radical in manner and sentiment and goes for universal reform, toleration, and almost universal suffrage. He compared Lord Derby to a French juggler. He declared that the Church of England was in a most unhappy condition, mentioned various items that had been expended on the Bishops' residences, and said he should respect any Bishop far more who would travel about the country on horseback with a pair of saddle-bags. In fact, he talked very much as one would imagine ultra-American Democrats to speak of England. He had very able and conclusive opponents in Lord William Powlett and Robert Clive, both of whom supported Lord Derby's administration, still reserving for themselves an independent action in case of necessity. I fancy my mother must be disappointed in Lord Derby's policy. Uncle Richard gave the clearest and most concise reasons for it that I have heard; that is, that Lord Derby sees the impossibility of restoring the duty on corn and that all that he can do is to lift some burden from the land equivalent to the increased remuneration which the duty on corn would give.

The tithes and poor rates are immense, the former particularly so upon this estate. For example, Mr. Ridgeley rents a farm of four hundred acres of the Moor property, for which he pays two pounds an acre, and upon this his church and poor rates amount to sixty pounds. This whole estate pays four hundred pounds for tithes alone, and the poor rates are immense. Were Lord Derby to attempt to restore the duty upon corn, he would not remain in office an hour. Robert Clive made an admirable speech, clear and manly and delivered without hesitation or embarrassment. Lord William Powlett, though a clever person, has such a terrible nervous affection of the face that one listens to him with no pleasure. We were very much interested in Robert Clive's success, as you may imagine, as he is so shy and dreamy that we doubted it.

To-day, Thursday, the husting takes place, and to-morrow the successful candidates are chaired and cheered. They are carried through the town in chairs, and otherwise, I suppose, made much of. All this is a bore to Robert Clive, who would rather sit cross-legged and smoke, or paint.

Yesterday afternoon Aunt C. and I went into a shoe-shop and there we found Lord William Powlett and a clergyman from Clee Hill, Mr. Brown, *alias* "Dodger" Brown, canvassing Mr. Venables's vote.

"No, sir," said Venables, "I shan't give you my vote. I have nothing to say against you, Lord Powlett, and Mr. Clive, as gentlemen, but your party, the Conservatives, have crushed me, and I am not going to give my vote to those who have taken the bread out of my mouth."

Here Mrs. Venables spoke. "All my husband's misfortunes are h'owing," said she, "to the Conservatives."

Then said Venables, "I always voted for the Conservatives until they crushed me, and I am not going to vote for them any more."

Lord Powlett and Mr. Brown tried to find out how they had crushed him, but he would not or could not say, but still he went on ascribing his misfortunes to the Conservatives, and we left the two gentlemen to argue it out with him. I felt mortified to see this elegant gentleman, Lord William, asking the vote and hearing the reproaches of a vulgar Radical.

We have not heard from Mr. Lowell yet. We were to have spent last Wednesday or Saturday of this week at Acton Scott with Mrs. Stackhouse-Acton, but she was ill and put us off until next week. Richard has been quite ill, but is now better.

XXII

MARIA was so kind, as I was rather behindhand in my letter, to let me send hers to you before sending it to my grandfather. She has seized various opportunities of writing when I have been asleep. Two cups of coffee last night have produced one sheet for her, and a flea having feasted on me has forced me to get up this morning at seven o'clock. We have had, as you may suppose, a charming visit to Mrs. Stackhouse-Acton. The first day three beaux enlivened the scene. One of these was Mr. Wilson, who was as handsome as ever, and none the less so the next day when we saw him at his parsonage at Church Stretton. Here was the perfection of a country parson's life; a nice large house, a fine garden, exquisite scenery, and a pretty church hard by, schools, and loving parishioners, and something more than forty pounds a year. We also went to see Mrs. Acton's church, whose rector is a true Paddy and a bachelor, for who could marry on a hundred pounds a year?

He lives in a little cottage overgrown with vines, in rustic style, and a pretty garden adorned the front of the house, taken care of by himself. As we came round at the back of the house, we surprised him at work in his kitchen garden. He welcomed us with true Irish cordiality, took us into his house and showed us some carvings in wood, an accomplishment with which he solaces himself after the labors of the day are over.

Wednesday we spent at Wenlock Abbey, some ten miles from Acton Scott. We drove there early in the morning through the most beautiful country, first uphill, then along the top of a chain of hills called Wenlock Ridges, looking down on a rich valley, the Stretton mountains rising above us on the other side. We saw the Wrekin, a mountain so beloved of the Salopians that it has given rise to a toast — "All friends round the Wrekin."

At last we reached Wenlock, where we sat down to sketch the ancient and picturesque ruins of the Abbey. I made a very successful sketch that I shall be proud to show you. Mrs. Acton is most liberal with her drawings, and has given me no less than three. We lunched at the rector's house, the most romantic place possible, and the rector showed us the church, parts of which are very ancient, and also the market-place. Thus we passed a charming day and reached home for dinner at half-past seven o'clock. Yesterday morning we spent in looking over Mrs. Acton's innumerable drawings and beautiful books, and I began to copy a sketch of hers. She says we may take anything we choose to the Moor to copy. There is no end to her kindnesses, and, besides, she is exceedingly agreeable and has had a most varied experience, and has many accomplishments.

The house is Elizabethan, and everything corresponds; even the wine-glasses are in that style. Everywhere the hand of the artist is evident, while the whole place is in perfect order and taste. She is a sister of the late Lady Boughton, and her father was a great botanist, the owner of Downton Castle.

Aunt C. and Uncle R. drove over to lunch and took us back with them. Richard has been so ill that we should not have left him had he not been on the way to recovery. It seems almost decided that we shall go home with the Lowells on August 21st, and Aunt C. has written to ask them to come and make a visit at the Moor on their way to Liverpool.

XXIII

My dear Mother:

The common letter from Acton Scott has reached
you ere this. In the meantime I received your
letter which expresses so much anxiety for my return. There was nothing left for me to do but to
wait, for our passages had already been taken on
the steamer of the 21st of August. We are to go out
under the care of Mr. and Mrs. Frank Lowell, and
they have been invited to take the Moor on their
way to Liverpool. Mr. and Mrs. George Baty
Blake go in the same steamer with us and to
Boston. At this season we are likely to have fine
weather, and it is hardly probable that we shall be
ill.

Richard left to-day to go to the seashore, and
perhaps to Ireland. He has just recovered from his
long illness. It seems strange that leading, as he
has done, a life so regular and healthful, he should
not have gained, rather than have lost, health. He
has not been well since March, and I think the
seeds of the malady were laid in Germany. He
comes home the first of October, returning to the
Moor for partridge shooting. At this season in
England picnics are the rage, and the more inaccessible the place chosen and the greater the

obstacles to be overcome, the greater is supposed to be the pleasure.

In this case the highest point of the Clee Hill, Tilteston by name, was selected, and as it is some nineteen hundred feet above the sea, you can fancy some effort necessary to reach the top. The carriage took us some eight or ten miles, but not the least of our troubles was where and how to find the party; for stopping at Mr. James's, a clergyman, halfway up, they told us that the others had preceded us an hour and a half, but how they had gone no one knew. Whether we could drive, or whether we must walk some three miles, remained a mystery we ourselves must solve. There stood Tilteston, wild and barren even of a stone that would cast a shadow in the midsummer sun. In vain we looked; Tilteston gave back no sign that a creature lived on its desolate summit. All that remained for us was to push on, for besides the attainment of pleasure, unappeased appetite began to raise a cry for Tilteston. We were fain to sit down by the wayside and crouch under the shade of a solitary stone that at intervals marked the way — affording the only shade in all this vast expanse, save here and there a black mound cast up from some coal pit — and enjoy the contents of our basket, but a lingering hope of at length finding the party prevailed, and we drove slowly on until the carriage would take us no farther.

At this extremity a collier came running towards

us and told us he could show us the way. The basket was transferred from the carriage to his shoulders, and then began our ascent, now uphill, now through a morass, now looking up and seeing our goal, as we thought, pushing on with renewed vigor and energy through the heather and nettles, at length reaching the desired point and finding two more ascents necessary, every moment our faces getting redder and our empty stomachs crying more lustily. However, all things have an end, and at length we stood on the summit and looking down beheld the party seated in a hollow that looked as if it had been made by some giant taking out stones to amuse himself by rolling them down the mountain.

The party were seated on the ground around a tablecloth upon which were the débris of pigeon, rabbit, and veal pasties, cold meats of all sorts, and various tarts, to say nothing of empty bottles. Notwithstanding the devastation already made, the work of destruction was still going on; every face was gazing earnestly upon a plate, and such red faces! the sun evidently having fixed the color the walk had given.

Gentlemen immediately came to our assistance and seated us comfortably and began to provide for our wants, but alas! we had our troubles even then. My plate rested on my lap. I put a delicious piece of pigeon-pie into my mouth, but the sun broils me, and I seize my parasol in one hand and my glass of champagne in the other. Incontinently a shepherd dog comes putting his nose into my plate. I drop my parasol, which flies off, upsetting Uncle Richard's champagne in its way. I drive the dog off and am forced to drink the whole glass of wine because there is no place to put it. Soon a currant tart tempts me, and I ask Aldersey, handing him my plate, to get me some.

"What is to be done, Miss Fay?" said he, "there is no clean plate to be had. The dogs have put their noses into the pail of water, and there is only one resource, my dog, Crab," said he with a significant look. He calls Crab, disappears with the plate, and comes back with it looking very nicely licked. I have my prejudice, however, and suggest that I shall use the bottom of the plate, but then there is a doubt about keeping the juice of the currant pie from running over, and so the discussion was at length ended by Aldersey seeing some plates covertly lying in a basket and making a dash at them and triumphantly brings one off.

"Now," says he, "Miss Fay will have some currant tart without straw," for I had been helped to pigeon-pie with hay. The repast is at length over and the gentlemen retire to smoke and the ladies sit down to gossip. We should have found sufficient to enjoy in the magnificent view which commands nineteen counties, but, alas! a November-like fog left us only the desolate point upon which we stood.

When the gentlemen got through smoking, it

was time for us to descend. We are to go to Mr. James's to dance. We are to go straight down the face of the mountain, and with Aldersey's assistance I begin the descent, but such a guide as I have! Assuming the mountain a slide, he leads, drawing me after him. It was impossible to walk, I must run. He takes everything and I must follow, for the heather and turf are so slippery that I am utterly helpless, hence I come to grief, but I am hurried on until we reach the bottom.

You can fancy that after three miles of such a walk we do not feel very much like dancing, but we have it to do and I am only too thankful when I find myself once more at the Moor. This is pleasure! There is a picnic talked for next week at Downton Castle, which is perfectly accessible, and without doubt will be very pleasant.

This is the last time you will hear from me. Two weeks after this you will receive me after eleven months' absence.

XXIV

Katharine Fay to her Aunt Maria Fay

MY DEAREST PET:

I have been waiting a long time to write to you, for I thought you would rather hear from me at Shropshire than anything else, and now I have just come home from a charming visit there. In the first place, you must know that Willie brought me over to Louise Cannon's in time for the Hereford Music Meeting. We went over and slept at the Green Dragon and spent the day at the Cathedral, hearing oratorios. The music was excellent and the Cathedral, which has been restored, very beautiful. I cannot fancy why English people rush after churches on the Continent, when they have so much more beautiful ones at home. Except Milan Cathedral and Cologne, I have seen nothing superior to the English churches, even the few I know. They are spoiled by tinsel and trumpery, Cologne not so much as Milan.

We saw the Keville-Davises, Lord Bateman and Mr. Hanbury and his wife, and Tom Dunn and some other old neighbors. Then we came back to a quiet interval which we spent in reading, sewing,

walking, and, would you believe it? in taking singing lessons. I cannot tell you how much I enjoyed
them. Before I forget it, let me recommend you to
read Lord Stanhope's "Life of Pitt." You will find
it most entertaining and agreeable.

The other day we went to Shropshire to make
a visit at Clungunford (John Roache's), and who
should be among the party to receive us but Miss
Beale, looking very well and not a day older than
when you saw her.

She sings and plays as much as ever, and is, in
fact, perfectly unaltered in every way. The second
day after we arrived was the Ludlow Agricultural
Show, and it being Fair Day we all piled in on a
large carriage and took posters to go there. We
drove to the Angel for lunch and were regaled with
hot chops and beer, after which I proceeded out
into Broad Street. The first person I espied was
Mr. Betton, looking very spruce and well-dressed.
I went up and said, "How do you do, Mr. Betton,"
upon which he said, "Don't tell me who it is, let
me see if I can remember." However, he could not
remember, and Miss Beale came to his assistance.
He was very much delighted and inquired for all
the family. He then said that he wished to intro-
duce me to his wife. After a chat, I left him and
Miss Beale.

The next person I stumbled on was Mr. Bridges,
grayer, but still looking very much as he did. Then
I thought I should go to old Mr. Jones's shop; do

you remember it? It had not the attractions of Partridge's and always excited my sympathies in consequence. He was very much pleased at not being forgotten and sold me ten shillings' worth of photographs of Ludlow, with great pleasure. Then over to Partridge's, who has a very fine new shop with every conceivable thing in it. Partridge himself is unchanged, except that he is very much interested in the volunteer movement, and has a large, black moustache. His cheeks are still red, and he gave me the news of Ludlow in the brisk, business-like way that you remember.

After seeing the cattle, which were exhibited in the castle yard, and chatting with the Keville-Davises, Mr. Luttrile Clark, Tom Dunn, and others, we proceeded to the church. It would do your heart good to see it. Without being made new-looking, it has been restored as nearly as possible to its original condition. The whitewash has been scraped away, the galleries removed, the pews lowered, the organ taken away from between the chancel and the nave, and, in fact, every attraction that good taste combined with veneration for antiquity could suggest. I send you a photograph of the interior which will give you a faint idea of the present aspect.

The chancel is left very much as you remember. After seeing the church, we went to the house of old Miss Beale, who once upon a time read the service for herself and another woman when the clergyman thought that two did not make a congregation. She is looking very well and does queer things still, to the amusement of her relations. She cannot conceive why every one, that can, does not live in Ludlow, and looks upon it as an immense privilege to live so near the church.

I found Mr. Betton sitting there with his new wife and she is very young and nice-looking. A few days after the Fair, I went to Oakly Park to meet Lady Windsor (formerly Lady Harriet Clive) who was staying there. At Bromfield the flags were all flying in honor of her arrival, and the Park looks even more beautiful than when I remember it. Do you recollect the variety of fine trees, and yet dear Lady Windsor always apologized for them and said she was sure they must look so small to me. Really, I never have seen any trees taller or more luxuriant, especially when one considers the different kinds and all of them such good specimens. I think I never saw anything more beautiful. Lady Mary (the widow of Robert Clive, who had died six years before) takes great interest in the trees and watches the Wellingtonias and deodars just as if they were children.

After lunch, we all took bill-hooks and saws and the two gentlemen axes and went out to cut the laurel where it had grown up too tall. Lady Mary, little Miss Clive, Victoria, and I worked till we were tired and then went on to the lawn to play croquet with the children (children of Robert

Clive). They are very dear little things and so well brought up. Little Bob (the present Lord Windsor) is just six years old and rides every day, and plays cricket very well for such a little thing. He is not at all spoiled and is to be sent to school when he is old enough, which I think is so wonderful when you consider that he is the youngest and only son and heir of the family. Lady Windsor is devoted to him and you would be amused to see them singing out of the same hymn-book and the little thing holding up his finger at her when he thinks she does not sing right. One afternoon, Lady Mary drove Bob and me to Ludlow Castle in her pony phaeton, the rest following in the carriage. We went by a new road which Robert Clive planned and which goes nearly all the way through the grounds back of the castle.

Victoria and I made a hasty sketch. In the evening we had music. Lady Mary has an "orgue expressive," and they have trios, Victoria playing on the piano and little Miss Clive on the concertina. You know they have always been devoted to music. There was a Mr. Wade, who is a very good tenor, and besides is a nice, cultivated person, so is very much sought after in country houses. We used to keep him singing in a relentless manner.

On Sunday evening, as a great treat, Lady Mary took us to church at Ludlow. Generally the horses are not taken out. You have no idea how beautiful the church is at night. They had a choir of boys and men and excellent music; also we heard a very good sermon from Mr. Myrick, and the rector is still the same as when we were at the Moor.

A delightful institution in England is the five o'clock tea, just come up. Before dressing for dinner we all used to assemble in Lady Mary's morning room, where there are nothing but very low and comfortable seats, and drink tea and eat thin bread and butter. It is so refreshing after being out all the afternoon. Several times we looked through Robert Clive's Eastern sketches. How very clever and artistic they are. It makes me feel a new desire to go on.

Now I believe I have told you everything I can think of about everything and everybody. Mrs. Hussey (formerly Miss Clive) has not only twins, but still adds to her family. Lady Powis's sight is no longer indifferent as she has had an operation performed and can see very well. I wish you would come and look up the old places again next spring. Every one inquires for you with great interest.

Lady Windsor talked about you in a way that would have made your ears burn. She is much softened without losing her dignity of manner and is very tender and affectionate. She finds it a great trial to see Oakly Park twice bereft of two heads, her husband and her son, and is now only a visitor there, though a most welcome and honored one. She and Lady Mary are most devoted to each other.

Now my paper brings me to a conclusion. I do hope you will cross the Atlantic in the spring and see some more of the beautiful things on this side. It is enough to drive a sketcher wild if she or he has not time to stop and draw everything that is pretty.

THE END

250

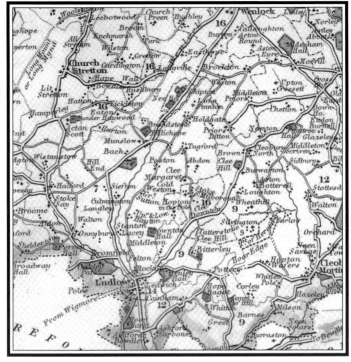

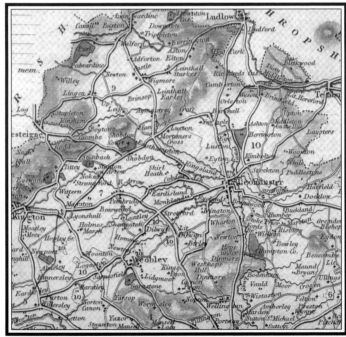

South Shropshire and North Herefordshire -
Thomas Moule c. 1830

Afterword

The Fay Family

The Preface of this book gives brief details about Anna Maria's life, but these do not do justice to the large and interesting family that she came from. Further information has emerged from research carried out by the members of the Fay family.

Anna Maria's grandfather, Judge Samuel Prescott Phillips Fay, was born in June 1778 in Concord, Massachusetts, the eldest son of Jonathan Fay and his wife Lucy Prescott. The unusual fact, for the Fay family, that he had two middle names indicates his strong sense of family and their roots. He graduated from Harvard in the same class as Stephen Longfellow, the father of the poet. After graduation he was commissioned into the American Army and was stationed at Oxford, Massachusetts. Although he remained in the army during the French wars of 1798 and 1799 he did not see active service. After the successful second peace mission sent to France by President Adams, the army was disbanded and Samuel Fay began to study law. When he had completed his studies and been admitted to the bar, he opened an office in Cambridge, Massachusetts. He was soon a successful lawyer and in 1821 was appointed Judge of Probate for Middlesex County, Massachusetts. He held this office for thirty five years until March 1856 when ill health forced him to resign. He was a member of the Governor's Council in 1818 and involved in constitutional affairs for Massachusetts, as well as Harvard College. He died in 1856; he 'was universally esteemed and respected, and by his death the bar lost one of its most honourable and valued members.'[1]

Judge Fay and his wife Harriet Howard had seven children. Samuel Howard, Anna Maria's

1. Maria Denny Fay

father, was the oldest and her aunt, Maria Denny, who travelled to Ludlow with her, was second youngest child. As she was born in 1820, she was only eight years older than Anna Maria. She was educated at the Ursuline Convent in Charlestown, Massachusetts. Like her niece, she did not marry but remained at home with her parents at what was later to be called Fay House in Cambridge, Massachusetts, where they lived from 1835-1859. Maria showed the same desire to travel as her niece. An unpublished diary of 1835 relates her travels, with friends, by stage coach, canal boat and steamer through New York State to Niagara Falls and into Canada.[2]

Her mother, Harriet Howard, died in 1847 and her father in 1856 and in 1885 Maria sold the house to the Society for the Collegiate Instruction of Women, which later became Radcliffe College and the Radcliffe Institute of the University of Harvard.

Fay House

Fay House had been bought by Judge Fay from the Higginson family who described him as 'a picturesque character, like the English sporting gentleman of the illustrated papers, who might be seen riding out of his stables of a fine day in search of the game that was to be found in the vicinity of the town at the time.'[3] The house was 'a centre of hospitality'[4] where the family received a wide circle of friends, including many people from the literary world, often entertained by music as Maria Denny was an accomplished musician. 'Miss Fay was a friend to all the world, and the old house was always full of nephews and nieces, sick people and well people, who had come to accept her hospitality.'[5]

The house had been built by Nathaniel Ireland in 1807 and had a 'sense of agreeable amplitude: the halls are spacious, the staircase broad, and the landings ... of generous width and lighted by triple windows, from which one catches delightful views of the town below and the countryside beyond.'[6] It also had a dignity, a certain faded elegance, a flavour of the old world.'[7] These descriptions of Fay House, which Anna Maria must have known well, help us to understand her appreciation of the English country houses that she visited.

**2. Fay House
Harvard
USA**

Anna Maria Fay

Anna Maria's father, Samuel Howard, was born in 1804 in Cambridge and married Susan Shellman in Savannah, Georgia in 1825. He died at the comparatively young age of forty three in 1847 in Brooklyn, New York. Anna Maria's mother lived until she was seventy nine and died in 1887. Samuel and Susan had five children. Anna Maria's siblings, Harriet, Willie, Susy and Clara are mentioned in the letters with special affection, so it must have been a great sadness to her when Susy died two years after the letters from England were written.

Anna Maria was the eldest of the family. Next came Harriet who married the Rev. James Smith Bush. They lived in West New Brighton, Staten Island, New York and had four children. After a gap, William Gaston was born in 1838; he married Emma Courtney Fenner and they had four children, including twins. Susan Elliott was born in 1842 and died in New Haven, Connecticut at the age of twelve and the youngest child was Clara Montfort, born in 1845. She married Frank Hill Smith[8] in 1874. They had four children and it must have been after the birth of the youngest, Clarence, in February 1881, that she died and Anna Maria, at the age of fifty three, came to look after her niece and nephews. Because Anna Maria was unmarried, this move seems to have caused some gossip at the time. Boston-born Frank was an artist and an architect and 'decorated numerous public and private buildings in both Boston and Cambridge ... He was a director of the school of the Boston Museum of Fine Arts.' Joseph Story Fay, Anna Maria's uncle, owned land in Woods Hole, Massachusetts and gave forty acres of land to another niece, Laura Greenough Ripka. Frank designed a house, in 'Shingle Style', for the site in 1885 and also redesigned a Colonial house in Falmouth as a 'Shingle Style' home. It is thought that Anna Maria was given the house by her Uncle Joseph for her lifetime but it was to be left to Clara and Frank's four children after her death.[9]

Some twenty five years after her return to America, Anna Maria wrote an article for the New England Historical and Genealogical Register called 'Some Account of the Life and Times of the Rev. Peter Bulkeley'.[10]

Letters written to John Jay Chapman, essayist and moralist, by Anna Maria at an advanced age ('by a veteran lady of more than 80'), reveal her as articulate, well read, thoughtful and interested in politics and philosophy. Her own interest in writing, caught in a reference to her own 'two Idylls, one in the Spencerian stanza and one in Blank verse,' is reflected in her admiration of his style: '''Dull''! No indeed! I found yr little book delightful.' A very graceful compliment to a friend of hers who encouraged her to publish is followed by the matter of fact 'I write no more as four infant orphans of my sister fell to my care. I had to desert idealism.'

Remarking on another part of Chapman's work, Anna Maria refers to the sight of a Negro woman being sold in a slave market in a Southern town in around 1836. She wrote how this troubled her eight year old conscience, following this statement with the puzzling 'I consoled myself with the thought that Negroes had not the same feelings as white people.' The reader wishes that one might see more of her thoughts on this subject to understand what this meant to her. Chapman himself, of course, was the grandson of Maria Weston Chapman, who was one of the leading campaigners against slavery and worked with William Lloyd Garrison on *Liberator*. This helps to explain Chapman's interest in Garrison, to which Anna Maria refers. Anna Maria's reference to Lord Rosebery and Lord Chatham show her familiarity with English politics, Rosebery having written more than one thing about William Pitt. [11]

One feels her regret at being able now to read only 'laboriously for myself, my sight being none too good.' It is fortunate that she had friends to read for her and correspondents to discuss what she had read.

In 1900 she was sharing an apartment with her niece, Rosamund Hill Smith. She is described as head of the house and a 'capitalist' but by 1920 Rosamund has become the head of the house and there is no occupation given for either woman. Two years later Anna Maria died.

Richard Sullivan Fay

Another of Anna Maria's uncles, Richard Sullivan, was born in 1804. He graduated from Harvard and lived in Boston where he was a merchant. He owned a summer estate in Lynn, Massachusetts which is idyllically described in his biographical notes. 'The situation is delightful. The little lake which has received the pretty name, 'Lynnmore' nestles so cosily and smiles so brightly between the thickly wooded hills, that it might almost be imagined there had been a compact that it should be shielded from the wild winds that agitate its bosom in return for the refreshing exhalations it might send up to renovate the dropping foliage.'[12] Richard planted many rare trees to beautify the estate where the family went every summer.

Richard married Catherine Saunders Pickman of Boston in 1832 and they had four children, who were all in England with the family. Richard Sullivan junior, born in 1833, was Anna Maria's companion on many Shropshire rides.

Later in his life he was on the staff of General Butler of Virginia during the early years of the Civil War. Katherine, or Kitty, born in 1837, married Sidney Everett who became secretary of the American Legation in Berlin, Germany, in 1883. William was aged twelve in 1851 and Elizabeth, the youngest child, only ten. They both married and had families. Uncle Richard died, like his brother, at the young age of fifty nine in Liverpool. Despite the ill-health recounted by Anna Maria, Aunt Catherine survived him and lived on to a respectable age.

There is no information about why Uncle Richard came to England and how he came to Moor Park. It would seem that he wanted to escape the harsh New England winters and during his stay he seems to have enjoyed relatively good weather at all seasons, as recorded by Anna Maria. It would be interesting to know how he made contact with the Salweys and arranged to rent the house[13]. The Lodge, an 18th century house nearby, also belonged to the Salweys and was rented out to the Bridges. (page 23)

The American family must have seemed like exotic birds in the quiet backwater that this corner of Shropshire was then. This is shown by the eagerness with which the local gentry wanted to entertain them and to find out about their native country. A voyage across the Atlantic was not something to be undertaken lightly, despite the impression given by Uncle Richard's sudden decision to return to the States on business.

Anna Maria gives us a valuable eyewitness account of life, travel, entertainment and worship in Shropshire and Herefordshire in the middle of the 19th century.

Ludlow Assembly Rooms

The Assembly Rooms in Ludlow, which are still used for entertainment today, were opened on 2 July, 1840 on the site of the timber-framed White Horse Inn. These Rooms were the venue for the Race Ball and replaced the rather dilapidated Assembly Rooms on the top of the Market Hall, although this survived until 1887. Adjacent is the former Museum of the Ludlow Natural History Society which is now part of the Assembly Rooms' complex.

Anna Maria describes a 'Fair-day' in Ludlow 'around the market-house' in Castle Square. (page 15) Today the May Fair is held every year in the same place; in front of the Assembly Rooms, around the Square and down Mill Street.

The theatre in Ludlow was at the lower end of Mill Street and had 'a plain exterior but

3. The Assembly Rooms today

neat within.'[14] A company performed there every year during race week and came to the town for two months every three years.

Ludlow Church

Anna Maria gives a good and appreciative description of the church but she is not quite correct in calling the style Early English (pages 16 and 19) as much of the building is 15th century and therefore Perpendicular. However, there is work from earlier periods going back to about 1200 and the unusual hexagonal porch is in the 14th century Decorated style.

4. The Assembly Rooms with the May Fair

Anna Maria shows a keen interest in church organs so that she can pass on the information to her family. The organ in Ludlow is a fine one made by John Snetzler, a famous 18th century organ builder. At the time of her visit it was on top of the screen dividing the nave from the choir of this former collegiate church. The Rev. Robert Meyrick was one of the curates and the reader for Ludlow Parish Church and lived

5. Interior of St. Laurence's Church, Ludlow 1840

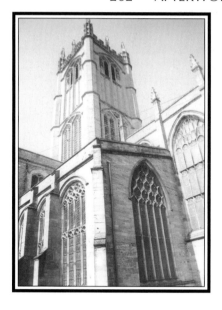

6. St. Laurence's Church

at Dinham Lodge, Ludlow; he and his wife had five children. Anna Maria and her family went to dinner with him in January 1852.

Richard's Castle Church

The parish of Richard's Castle is in two counties and the church Anna Maria knew is in Herefordshire. It has a Norman nave and a bell tower of about 1300. The plaster that she mentions with such horror (page 39) was originally put on to cover up and help preserve the rather poor stone that is found in that area. A new church was built at nearby Batchcott, in the Shropshire part of the

7. Richard's Castle Church, c. 1830

parish, in 1891 by the architect Norman Shaw. The old church has since been made a redundant church but is open for visitors. The Rev. George Landon lived at the Rectory at Batchcott with his large family – Charles, Agnes, Emma, Edward, Henry, Ernest, Janet, Kate and Reginald. It is now a private house.

8. The Old Rectory, Batchcott today

Burford Church

This church is noted both for its historically interesting monuments and for the major restoration work carried out in 1889 by the architect, Sir Aston Webb, in what is described as 'a free Arts and Crafts Gothic'.[15] This is long after Anna Maria's time, although some work had just taken place as she says. Among the many fine monuments in the church are some wall tablets to the Misses Rushout who Anna Maria meets on several social occasions.

9. Burford Church today

Clipper Ships, Inns and Steam Trains

Anna Maria arrived at Liverpool aboard the sailing packet *Parliament*. It was 1200 tons and was owned by the White Diamond Line of Enoch Train of Boston. The fleet of the White Diamond Line, despite the loss of two of her ships, had a reputation for 'excellent sailing qualities and the fact that their cargoes always arrived in sound condition. Their excellent sailing qualities surpassed the finest New York packets...' The

length of the journey in 1851 was around fourteen days. The ships, including the *Parliament*, were built by Donald McKay, a renowned builder of fine ships.[16]

The days of the sailing ships were numbered as steam would soon replace them and Anna Maria mentions receiving a letter from her family 'by British steamer'. (page 193) She had travelled to Ludlow on the mail coach which 'put them down before the Angel Inn', one of the two posting houses in Ludlow; the other was the Crown in Broad Street. Anna Maria was keen to see The Feathers, Ludlow's grandest

**10. The
Angel
Inn, Ludlow**

inn with 'its antique front and beautiful carving'. (page 29) This ancient building has been an inn since the 17th century.

During her visit, the first steam train arrived in Ludlow and when she goes to Shrewsbury for the races she travels on the

newly arrived railway. It took two hours to travel the twenty seven miles, compared with the four

11. The Feathers Hotel 1868

and a half hours for the mail coach. The train stopped at ten stations or halts: Bromfield, Onibury, The Craven Arms, Wistanstow, Marshbrook, Little Stretton, Church Stretton, Leebotwood, Dorrington and Condover. The line remains today but the only stops are Craven Arms and Church Stretton.

12. The Feathers Hotel today

The Three Choirs Festival

This festival is considered to be one of the oldest in the world and is held annually in the cathedral cities of Hereford, Gloucester and Worcester in rotation. It was started in 1715, but its present form dates from 1724 as a means of raising money for charity. The festival lasts over several days and is held in venues around the cathedral cities. Church choral music was and still is a major part of the programme.

Racecourses

At the time of Anna Maria's visit, Shrewsbury Racecourse was on the east of the town on land provided by the Earl of Tankerville on his Whitehall estate. The first meeting was held in 1832. In 1837, Thomas Carline, of the Shrewsbury family of builders and architects, had designed a

13. Grand-stand at Ludlow Racecourse today

new grandstand modelled on one at Wolverhampton. John Frail, at one time a hairdresser, was Clerk of the Course from 1843-1879 and he made arrangements with the railways to put on special fares to Shrewsbury on race days. The Shrewsbury Racecourse Company survived until 1887 when it became bankrupt.

Ludlow Racecourse was laid out at Bromfield about 1739 and soon became the centre of a social week in the town. A grandstand was built in 1820. Although she considered the course to be 'one of the prettiest in England' Anna Maria did not go to the meeting at the end of June. (page 229)

Leominster held its annual horse races over two days, usually in September. The course was situated on the flat land to the south east of the town and was used until the railway cut through the centre in 1853. The Leominster Guide of 1808 wrote that 'The plates are confined to hunters bred in the county, galloways, and ponies; which generally maintain a severe contest, and afford excellent diversions'.[17] Anna Maria attended a steeplechase in April so it would appear that races were held at other times than just the September meeting. (pages 185-189)

NOTES

[1] Information from the Fay Family Website, courtesy of Linda Fay Kaufman.

[2] Information from the Fay Family Website.

[3] Information from the Fay Family Website.

[4] 'Fay House of Radcliffe College', Arthur Gilman, Harvard Graduates ' Magazine, June 1896.

[5] 'The Ghosts of Fay House', Mary Lee, The Radcliffe Quarterly, Vol XIII, No. 2, May 1929.

[6] Boston Evening Transcript, November 1, 1891.

[7] 'Fay House of Radcliffe College', Arthur Gilman, Harvard Graduates' Magazine, June 1896. This article also notes that in the basement of an addition to the house, 'the late Professor Sophocles kept his precious hens, when they were not in the inclosure (sic) he made for them in the backyard. These fowls were like personal friends to the old Greek, and the impression made upon a stranger when he spoke to them was peculiar, for he had named them after members of the family ...'

[8] The name later became one word as Hillsmith.

[9] Information from the Fay Family Website.

[10] For more information on this article see the Fay Family Website.

[11] The three letters are in the Houghton Library, Harvard University, ref: bMS Am 1854 (566-568). John Jay Chapman (1862-1933) is now considered as 'one of the few great American letter writers'. (Jacques Barzun in his Foreword to a new edition of Chapman's *Unbought Spirit*, published by University of Illinois Press in 1998).

[12] Information from the Fay Family Website.

[13] In *Ludlow: A Historic Town*, by David Lloyd and Peter Klein, Chichester, 1984, there is a suggestion that the Fay family were distantly related to the Salweys. This link has not been established yet.

[14] *A Guide to the Town of Ludlow*, 1821, p.11.

[15] *The Buildings of England, Shropshire*, Nikolaus Pevsner, 1958.

[16] Information from Celia Underhill, *The American Neptune*, Volume 55, Number 3, Summer 1995 and the website, 'Era of the Clipper Ships', by Donald Gunn Ross III.

[17] *The Leominster Guide*, The Rev. Jonathan Williams, Leominster, 1808, reprinted 2000. We are grateful to Peter Holliday, Leominster Library, for supplying this information.

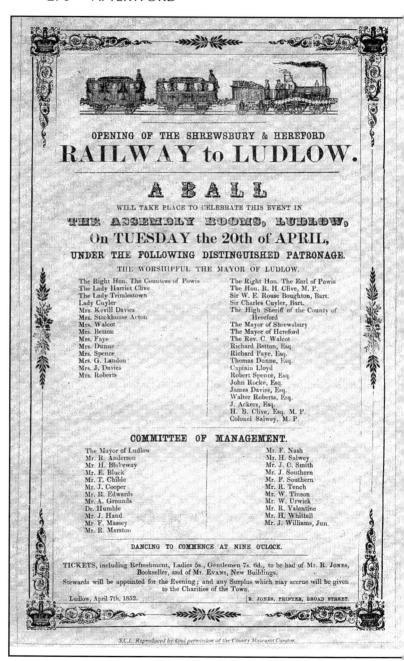

14. Announcement of the Ball, 1852

'In Valleys of Springs of Rivers'

The part of England that Anna Maria visited, South Shropshire and North Herefordshire, was made famous by the poet A. E. Housman in *A Shropshire Lad* and it is still a rural area with farming one of the main activities. The Shropshire Hills combine with small ancient towns and river valleys, to form a landscape of great beauty.[1]

Ludlow, as the largest town in the area, is the main centre with regular livestock sales and a town market held on three days each week all through the year. She would have recognised many of the buildings she describes. Shrewsbury, in the centre of Shropshire, is the main county town and a lively, attractive place. Although it still retains many of its splendid timber-framed buildings, others were swept away in post-war redevelopment.

Some of the places that Anna Maria visited are described in more detail below.

15. The Moor
c. 1830

Moor Park

Moor Park, where Anna Maria stayed during her English visit, belonged to the Salwey family, not Salway as she calls them in her letters. In the late 17th century, the Salweys purchased nearby Elton Hall and the Moor, as it was originally known, from the Littletons of Henley Hall. Richard Salwey moved into the Moor in 1721 and,

16. Moor Park today

after building work had taken place, it became the principal residence of the family.

'The general beauty of this charming residence has lately been greatly encreased (sic) by the improvements of the present tasteful and liberal owner.'[2] The identity of the architect is not known, although some sources attribute it to the prolific output of the Smiths of Warwick. This basically Queen Anne house has been altered and added to over the years. Anna Maria describes vividly the antiquity of the family and the old house and its contents. (pp.10-12) The building remained in the Salwey family until 1873. The building is now a school and has been extended to accommodate the activities there.

Oakly Park

Oakly Park is still the seat of the Earls of Plymouth, with the family name of Windsor Clive. It was originally an early 18th century house and was bought by Robert Clive of India in 1771 from the Earl of Powis. Anna Maria remarks on the involved relationship between the Clive and

17.
Oakly
Park
1830

Powis families on page 177 and there is a footnote explaining it further on page 14. Lady Harriet was born in 1797 and so was 54 when Anna Maria met her. Her town house was 53 Grosvenor Street, and that of the Powis's 45 Berkeley Square, both in London.

It is thought to have been Clive of India's favourite residence out of the many that he owned. 'Here the picturesque traveller is gratified with interesting and luxuriant views of distant woods and plantations, and rich and fertile valleys bounded by variety of bold distant and near pleasing eminence.'[3]

18. Lady Harriet Clive 1860

The elegant but unadorned house is set off by its magnificent ancient trees and park overlooking the River Teme.

19. The Hon. Robert Henry Clive

In October 1774 Clive was directing operations in the park by the river when he was drenched in a downpour and caught a heavy cold. This set off a chain of old illnesses; the pain they caused probably led to his violent death, probably by his own hand, not long after.

His widow, Margaret, lived on for another forty three years and spent much of her time at Oakly 'which always seems to have been full of guests'.[4]

20. Oakly Park today

Work was carried out on Oakly between 1748 and 1758 with further additions in about 1800. Major work was carried out in about 1820 by C. R. Cockerell and it is this building that Anna Maria would have known.

Bromfield Gatehouse

21.
Bromfield
Gatehouse

Anna Maria describes the school over the gateway by Bromfield Church. (page 120) The church is all that remains of a Benedictine Priory

church, which was under the control of Gloucester Abbey. The Priory was dissolved in the 16th century and part of the church was incorporated into a private house.

The Gatehouse, dating back to the 14th century, is the survivor of the Priory buildings.

Walcot Hall

Robert Clive bought the Walcot estate in 1764 from young Charles Walcot who sold it to settle debts; Clive paid £90, 000 for it. With the possession of Walcot, Oakly and other estates, Clive commanded a swathe of land

WALCOT.

along the Welsh Borders. This land and his immense wealth, estimated then at £1 million, gave him and his family power over the Parliamentary seats of the area and in 1767 he wrote: 'We shall come very strong into Parliament this year – seven without opposition; probably one more.' The seats he controlled were Shrewsbury, Montgomery, Bishop's Castle 'with three other friends of relations in other parts of

22. Walcot Hall 1824

23. Walcot Hall today

the country'.[5] Clive enlarged the estate and employed the architect Sir William Chambers to extend the house: 'a substantial mansion, which is rather plain, built of brick with stone dressing, has a massive Doric portico, which is approached by a fine avenue of limes and other lofty trees'.[6]

There is a reference to the Indian bungalow, known as the Hermitage, which was 'a thatched roundhouse surrounded by a verandah'.[7] Sadly it is no longer there. Clive began planting the trees for the arboretum which is such a feature of the park today. The lakes which Anna Maria points out were dug out by French prisoners of war. (page 174)

Clive's son married the heiress of the last Earl of Powis and in 1804 the title was granted to him under a new creation. He owned Walcot for 65 years and during his time the elegant ballroom at the back of the house was added. He also built a series of hot-houses which Anna Maria comments on. (page 175-6) The house remained with the Clive family until 1933.

The organ that Anna Maria refers to was made by Samuel Green, a renowned English organ builder of the 18th century. (page 175) The expedition to the camp was to the Bury Ditches, a large and impressive iron age fortification near Bishop's Castle. (page 176)

Ludford House

Ludford House (page 105) is probably one of the most ancient of the houses visited by Anna Maria. It was originally the leper Hospital of St. Giles; St. Giles was the patron saint of lepers and so that

24. Ludford House

infection did not spread, the building was outside the town walls. After the Reformation, the Hospital passed into private hands, first the Foxe family and then the Charltons who had owned it since 1632. The Charltons married into the Lechmere family of Hanbury in Worcestershire as Anna Maria mentions. (page 105)

Anna Maria describes the two contrasting sides of Ludford House: from the road, it 'looks like a jail' and the other shows the 'profound repose, the park-like aspect of a remote country place'.

> *The building appears of great antiquity, except the south front, and has of late been greatly improved and beautified. The garden and shrubbery are elegantly disposed. The interior of the house has been greatly altered and newly furnished in a style that bespeaks excellent fancy and elegance of taste in the present owner.*[8]

25. Ludford House from the garden

Additions and renovations were carried out to the house in the middle of the 18th century but little has changed since Anna Maria's visit.

Henley Hall

Henley Hall belonged to the Knight family. About 1772 the property had been sold to the Knights by Lord Lilford and the date on the rainwater heads shows that work was carried out then, such as the Georgian staircase and the classical front door. Much of the house is from an earlier date and probably goes back to the early 17th century.

> *The interior is richly and well furnished. In the south front is a large park, sprinkled with excellent oaks and well stocked with fine deer. The gardens, plantations and walks about the house display considerable neatness and beauty; the river Ledwich running through the grounds adds considerably to the agreeableness of the charming scenery around.[9]*

26. Henley Hall

Sir Charles Cuyler leased Henley and lived there with his extensive family. The house at that time was owned by the Rev. Samuel Knight, vicar of Welwyn, who married one of the Cuyler daughters. Sir Charles was a major general in the Army in the 59th Foot and had another local connection as his wife was a daughter of the Rev. Fitzwilliam Halifax, who had been a rector of Richard's Castle. They had seven daughters, including Anna Maria's friend, Constance, who married John Rocke (variously spelt Roche or Roache by Anna Maria) of Clungunford in 1853.

Sir Charles, who died in 1862, was a noted sportsman; for a wager, he was reputed to have shot twenty partridges with as many shots, without killing a hen or a young bird. After he left, Henley Hall fell into some disrepair and was sold out of the Knight family to Edmund Thomas Wedgewood Wood and it remains with the same family today.

Downton Hall and Downton Castle

When Anna Maria visited Downton Hall, Sir William Rouse Boughton was a widower; his wife Charlotte had died in 1842. She was one of the daughters of Thomas Andrew Knighton of Elton, Herefordshire and niece of Richard Payne Knight of nearby Downton Castle. Her father was a distinguished horticulturalist and developer of varieties of fruit and her uncle was renowned for his championing of the Picturesque movement. He built an innovative asymmetrical castle at Downton and landscaped the dramatic gorge of the River Teme according to his own principles. Richard

Payne Knight gave the estate to his brother and then it passed to Charlotte and through her to her husband and their second son. The family became

27. Sir William Rouse Boughton

28. Downton Hall 1831

29. Downton Hall today known at one time as Rouse Boughton Knight. At the time of Anna Maria's visit Downton Castle was empty as Thomas Andrew's widow had died in 1847. (pages 101-3)

The estate still belongs to descendants of the Rouse Boughton family. However, in the late 18th century a Boughton married Catherine Pearce, heiress of Downton Hall. The estate was originally owned by Serjeant Hall and then Wredenhall Pearce who built a brick house on the site in about 1738. The house was extended by his son ten years later and then more work

30. Downton Castle c. 1830

was carried out after 1824 by Sir William Rouse Boughton. The dining room, with its ornate plasterwork that Anna Maria admired so much, is still a feature of the house. (page 100)

31. Downton Castle today

Downton Hall stands on a magnificent site overlooking the Clee Hills, and in particular Titterstone Clee, not Tilteston as Anna Maria calls it.[10] The Clee Hills divide Shropshire from the Midlands and are an outstanding natural feature.

Acton Scott

Frances Stackhouse Acton was the sister of Charlotte Rouse Boughton. She married Thomas Stackhouse and their home was Acton Scott Hall near Church Stretton, Shropshire, a late 16th century gabled brick mansion. She was born in 1794 and was a lady of talent and energy,

32. Mrs Frances Stackhouse Acton c. 1870

**33. Acton
Scott
Hall
c.1870**

as Anna Maria indicates. Frances had worked
with her father, Thomas Andrew Knight, on his
horticultural projects, including supplying
drawings for him and had carried this passion into
her married life. The Stackhouses carried out
modernisation of their house, including the
addition of a dining room, a heated conservatory
and transformation of the gardens. They assumed
the additional name of Acton in 1834. Anna Maria
also visited the Rectory at Acton Scott, 'overgrown
with vines'. (page 235)

As Anna Maria discovered to her pleasure,
Frances was a keen artist who illustrated her book,
*The Castles and Old
Mansions of Shropshire*,
with her own drawings.

**34. The Rectory at Acton Scot.
c. 1870**

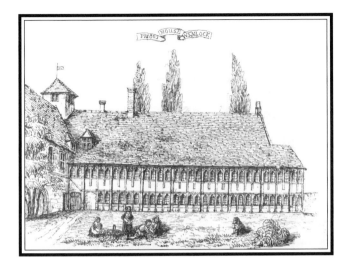

35. The Prior's House, Much Wenlock 1868

They enjoyed a day together sketching at Wenlock Priory, an important foundation dating from about 680 A.D. It was originally a nunnery with St. Milburga as its first abbess. The impressive ruins that are there today, in the care of English Heritage, date from several periods from 1150-1500.

The Prior's House or Lodge is one of the drawings in Frances Stackhouse Acton's book.[11] This very interesting building is described as 'one of the finest examples of domestic architecture in England, [dating from] about the year 1500'.[12] It is privately owned.

Stokesay Castle

The Great Hall at Stokesay Castle built was in the latter part of the 13th century and much of this splendid and romantic building dates from that time. It is one of the earliest fortified houses in England and was built by Laurence de Ludlow, a wealthy clothier, who was given permission to crenellate in 1291. The drawing by Frances Stackhouse Acton shows the south tower and the windows of the solar wing. She was concerned about the state of decay of the building and urged the owner at that time, Lord Craven, to restore it. The picturesque timber-framed Gatehouse is one of the Castle's most attractive features. Stokesay Castle is in the care of English Heritage and is open to the public.

36. Stokesay Castle, by Mrs Stackhouse Acton

Croft Castle

At the time of Anna Maria's visit, Croft Castle, Herefordshire, was occupied by the Keville Davies family. In the 18th century the Croft

family had mortgaged the estate to Richard Knight of Downton and he had called in the mortgage. Richard's daughter, Elizabeth, and her husband Thomas Johnes lived there until the latter part of the 18th century when Somerset Davies, a lawyer of Ludlow, took over the estate. They in turn became the Kevill Davies family.

37. Croft Castle 1907

Croft is a fortified house of the late 14th or early 15th century and still has the appearance of a castle. The building was given a new Gothick look in the middle of the 18th century by the Shrewsbury architect, Thomas Farnolls Pritchard.[13] Anna Maria comments on 'the modern parts' and on 'the beauty of the trees which form the avenue'. (pages 108-9) These are the famous ancient chestnuts of Croft.

The house is now the property of the National Trust and is open to the public.

38. Croft Castle oday.

Some Local Residents

Colonel Russell lived at Ashford Hall and Charles Joseph Russell, presumably his son, was an attorney at College Street in Ludlow and lived at 70, Linney; another of the family, Richard Russell, was an attorney in Broad Street. Lewin Luttrell Clark was also an attorney at 6 Mill Street, Ludlow. His brother, Philip, was his 'Gentleman Assistant'.[14] Miss Heightington, the dressmaker, was in Broad Street, Ludlow.

NOTES

[1] *A Shropshire Lad*, A. E. Housman, first published in 1896. The quotation is from Poem *L* '
'Clunton, Clunbury,
Clungunford and Clun,
Are the quietest places
Under the sun.'

[2] *A Guide to the Town of Ludlow*, 1821, p. 197.

[3] *A Guide to the Town of Ludlow*, 1821, p. 153.

[4] Information from *Clive of India*, Mark Bence-Jones, 1974 and *Clive*, Robert Harvey, 1998.

[5] Quoted in *Walcot Hall*, a brief history by the Woodbine Parish Family of Walcot, 1991.

[6] *The County Seats of Shropshire*, Francis Leach, 1891.

[7] *Historic Parks & Gardens of Shropshire*, Paul Stamper, 1996.

[8] *A Guide to the Town of Ludlow*, 1821, p. 184.

[9] *A Guide to the Town of Ludlow*, 1821, p. 175.

[10] Anna Maria also refers to the Vignyles which are the High Vinnalls, the forest and hill rising above Moor Park.

[11] *The Castles and Old Mansions of Shropshire*, Frances Stackhouse Acton, Shrewsbury, 1868. Wenlock was in fact a Priory, not an Abbey as Anna Maria calls it.

[12] Shropshire, *The Buildings of England*, Nikolaus Pevsner, 1958.

[13] For further information on Croft Castle and the work of Pritchard, see *Thomas Farnolls Pritchard of Shrewsbury*, Julia Ionides, The Dog Rose Press, 1999.

[14] Information from 1851 Census.

List of Illustrations

Portrait of Clara Fay by her husband, Frank Hill Smith, c.1870. (Private Collection)
Moor Park, the original frontispiece in the 1923 publication
Page 250 Map of South Shropshire and North Herefordshire, Thomas Moule, c.1830.

1. Portrait of Maria Denny Fay. (Radcliffe Archives, Radcliffe Institute, Harvard University)
2. Fay House, Cambridge, Massachusetts, now part of Harvard University.
3. The Assembly Rooms, Ludlow, in Mill Street.
4. The Assembly Rooms, Ludlow, from the Square with the annual May Fair.
5. St. Laurence's Church, Ludlow, 1840, Edward Hodson the Younger. (Private Collection)
6. St. Laurence's Church, Ludlow, today.
7. Richard's Castle Church, c.1830. (Private Collection)
8. The Old Rectory at Batchcott, Shropshire, today.
9. The tower of Burford Church, Shropshire, today.

10. The Angel Inn, Ludlow.
11. The Feathers Hotel, Ludlow; a drawing by Mrs. Stackhouse Acton from her book, *The Castles and Old Mansions of Shropshire*, 1868. (Private Collection)
12. The Feathers Hotel, Ludlow, today.
13. The grandstands at Ludlow Racecourse.
14. Announcement of the Ball for the opening of the railway to Ludlow, 1852. (Shrewsbury Records and Research Centre)
15. The Moor, as it was known then, c.1830. (Private Collection)
16. Moor Park, Shropshire, today, showing the 19th and 20th century additions.
17. Oakly Park, Shropshire, J. F. Neale. c.1830.
18. Lady Harriet Clive, Baroness Windsor, 1860, Sir Francis Grant R.A. (Private Collection)
19. The Hon. Robert Henry Clive by Sir Thomas Lawrence. (Private Collection)
20. Oakly Park, Shropshire, today.
21. Bromfield Gatehouse, near Ludlow.
22. Walcot Hall, Shropshire, 1824.
23. Walcot Hall, Shropshire, today.
24. Ludford House, Ludlow, from the Ludlow to Hereford Road.
25. Ludford House, Ludlow, from the garden.
26. Henley Hall, Ludlow, Shropshire.

27. Sir William Rouse Boughton, Solomon Cole. (Private Collection)
28. Downton Hall, Shropshire, F. Page, 1831.
29. Downton Hall today.
30. Downton Castle, Herefordshire, in the 19th century by Mrs. Frances Stackhouse Acton. (Private Collection)
31. Downton Castle, Herefordshire, today.
32. Photograph of Mrs. Frances Stackhouse Acton, c. 1870. (Private Collection)
33. Acton Scott Hall, Church Stretton, Shropshire, 1878. (Private Collection)
34. The Rectory at Acton Scott, c.1870. (Private Collection)
35. The Prior's House, Much Wenlock, Shropshire; a drawing by Mrs. Frances Stackhouse Acton from her book, *The Castles and Old Mansions of Shropshire*, 1868. (Private Collection)
36. Stokesay Castle, Shropshire, in the 19th century. (Private Collection)
37. Croft Castle, Herefordshire, the south front in about 1907. (Private Collection)
38. Croft Castle, Herefordshire.
39. Bill of Fare for the opening of the railway to Ludlow, 1852. (Shrewsbury Records and Research Centre)

Photographs by Peter Howell unless otherwise indicated.

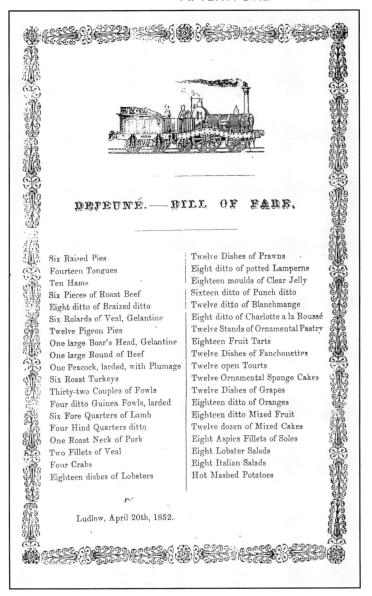

DEJEUNÉ.——BILL OF FARE.

Six Raised Pies
Fourteen Tongues
Ten Hams
Six Pieces of Roast Beef
Eight ditto of Braized ditto
Six Rolards of Veal, Gelantine
Twelve Pigeon Pies
One large Boar's Head, Gelantine
One large Round of Beef
One Peacock, larded, with Plumage
Six Roast Turkeys
Thirty-two Couples of Fowls
Four ditto Guinea Fowls, larded
Six Fore Quarters of Lamb
Four Hind Quarters ditto
One Roast Neck of Pork
Two Fillets of Veal
Four Crabs
Eighteen dishes of Lobsters

Twelve Dishes of Prawns
Eight ditto of potted Lamperns
Eighteen moulds of Clear Jelly
Sixteen ditto of Punch ditto
Twelve ditto of Blanchmange
Eight ditto of Charlotte a la Roussé
Twelve Stands of Ornamental Pastry
Eighteen Fruit Tarts
Twelve Dishes of Fanchonettes
Twelve open Tourts
Twelve Ornamental Sponge Cakes
Twelve Dishes of Grapes
Eighteen ditto of Oranges
Eighteen ditto Mixed Fruit
Twelve dozen of Mixed Cakes
Eight Aspics Fillets of Soles
Eight Lobster Salads
Eight Italian Salads
Hot Mashed Potatoes

Ludlow, April 20th, 1852.

39. Bill of Fare